FISHABLE
WRECKS
& ROCKPILES

BY TIM COLEMAN
& CHARLEY SOARES

MT PUBLICATIONS
P. O. BOX 211
TWO DENISON AVENUE
MYSTIC, CT 06355

CORRECTIONS

PAGE 7....43989.9 NOT 43899.9
PAGE 77...14283.8 NOT 14238.8
PAGE 113..43914.0 NOT 44914.0
PAGE 137..13362.2 NOT 13632.2

Library of Congress Cataloging-in-Publication Data

Coleman, Tim 1946-
    Fishable wrecks & rockpiles / Tim Coleman & Charley Soares
        p.   cm.
    ISBN 0-929775-01-5: $9.95
    1. Fishing — New England. 2. Shipwrecks — New England.
I. Soares, Charley, 1939-   . II. Title. III. Title: Fishable wrecks and rockpiles.
SH464.N48C65   1989
799.1´66346—dc20

                                                                89-28777
                                                                CIP

Copyright © 1989 by
All rights reserved.

MT PUBLICATIONS
Two Denison Avenue
Mystic, CT 06355

About This Book

If someone told an energetic fisherman that there are hundreds of productive reefs sitting off the New England coast going unfished in this day of the shrinking ocean, would that fisherman have his doubts? If he did, he'd be wrong for that's exactly what has happened, or should we say not happened, with sportfishing on shipwrecks.

Off our shores sit the remains of cargo ships, schooners, fishing trawlers and umpteen barges. All of these marine disasters, in time, became man-made reefs, attracting fish in moderate to large numbers. Yet for some reason, even in this day of inexpensive lorans, there are few fishermen targeting wrecks as potential fishing bonanzas.

This book should prove invaluable to an angler who wishes to take up wreck fishing since we've taken the guesswork out of the locations of ships. Once someone has the numbers, all he has to do is head to that spot and begin fishing.

Two years of hard research went into the preparation of Fishable Wrecks and Rockpiles. Many, many hours of that research were spent out where it counts the most, on the water verifying loran numbers. Other days were spent poring over back copies of newspapers and books, checking out details of the sinkings.

We hope to follow up this book with others like it as there's a lifetime of wrecks awaiting discovery. If you make a nice catch off one of the sites listed herein, we'd like to hear about it. Please drop us a line at MT Publications, Two Denison Avenue, Mystic, CT 06355.

Tim Coleman
Charley Soares

Contents

Contents

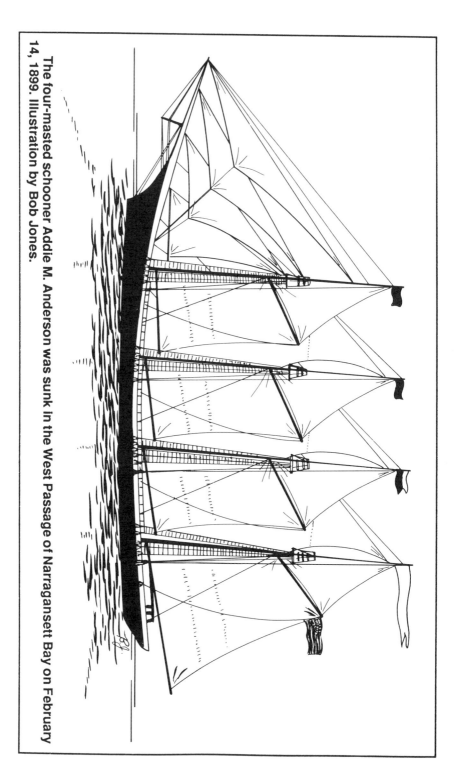

The four-masted schooner Addie M. Anderson was sunk in the West Passage of Narragansett Bay on February 14, 1899. Illustration by Bob Jones.

CHAPTER 1

Addie Anderson

On February 14, 1899 the four-masted schooner Addie M. Anderson rounded Montauk Point between the lighthouse and Great Eastern Rock. Halfway between those two landmarks she was stopped in her path by a submerged wreck. Prior to the collision her captain, James C. Tole, noted the ship was drawing 19 feet, 6 inches of water. He further declared he'd come through the same area before in other ships drawing 36 feet of water with the centerboard down. In between trips something or ship came to rest in previously safe waters. Later investigation indicated the wreck may have been the barge Star of the Sea which sank off Montauk Point the year before on November 27.

The Anderson was a wooden vessel, 183 feet long with a 38 foot beam. She was built in Bath, Maine in 1890 and homeported in New York. On the date of her sinking she was inbound from the Big Apple to Providence, R.I. with a cargo of coal.

Captain Tole and crew battled their leaking vessel and the cold all the way from Montauk to the entrance to the West Passage of Narragansett Bay. Around 1 a.m. on the 15th the ship arrived off Whale Rock off the town of Narragansett, R.I. By then it was apparent to Captain Tole that he could not save his ship. She was down by the bow and settling lower by the minute. With their vessel in danger of sinking from under them the captain and crew took to the lifeboats after hastily anchoring the ship.

The Anderson settled into roughly 50 feet of water. That morning her crew saw only the tops of the masts above the water after they were picked up by another schooner and taken to shore to be cared for. Six days after the sinking a wrecking crew determined the ship a total loss. As such she would be blown up to prevent her from becoming a hazard to navigation in this busy artery. The task of removing the wreck fell to the Army Corps of Engineers. In their Annual Report for 1899 they stated the hull, laying in mud and sand, was dynamited, giving a clearance at the time of 34 feet.

In September, 1968 Master Wreck Hunter Brad Luther of Fairhaven, Massachusetts dove on the remains of the Anderson and added it to his long list of located shipwrecks. Brad told me this ship used to be marked on older charts as a wreck but on a current chart you'll see an obstruction north of Whale Rock with clearance of 46 feet. That's the remains of the Anderson, the spot to fish.

Almost 90 years after her sinking, the bones of the Anderson showed up on the color fish finder of Captain Fred Gallagher's Kerritim as one finger of wreckage which was hard to stay on. After all those years there's not that much left at 14424.0 and 43899.9. I suspect the Anderson loads up with blackfish at times and could provide some jumbo fluke for those who drift around the site. Another fishing possibility would be to anchor near the wreck to fish pogy chunks on the bottom. You just might find some big blues stopping off on their way in and out of the bay.

Getting ready to cast around the wreck of the cement barge Angela on Old Cock Rock off Westport, Ma.

CHAPTER 2

Angela

You won't find many, if any, references to a "good wreck" but if there is one wreck which might fit that description it might be the Angela. Better known as the Cement Barge, she went aground and marked a most notorious reef and, further, did not cause any loss of life nor ecological damage as her cargo of cement mixed with the salt water and hardened.

Her weight and galvanized construction have helped her survive some brutal storms since she went aground on Hen and Chickens Reef off Westport, Ma. in 1971. She looks somewhat the worse for wear, her bright red exterior dulled but otherwise highly visible to mariners entering or leaving Buzzards Bay.

The Angela was one of three sister ships constructed by the Avondale Shipyard in New Orleans, La. from 1962 through 1963. The Atlantic Cement Company spent $9.6 million for the three ships named Angela, Adelaide and Alexander which were the largest ocean going barges in the world. They were 420 feet long, 80 feet wide and constructed of galvanized steel with a total capacity of 8,512 gross tons. All of this has contributed to the barge being able to withstand 18 hard years on the mean streets of the shipping lanes.

Toward the end of April of 1971, the Angela was loaded with 90,000 barrels of cement and towed by a Moran tug down the Hudson River to her first stop in Bayonne, N.J. She then continued down Long Island Sound bound for Boston via the Cape Cod Canal. On May 3rd seas began to build and the barge became so unmanageable she parted her heavy tow cable. In heavy weather and thick fog the barge was anchored very close to the reef while the tug headed to port to ride out the storm. When the weather abated the tug returned to find her charge high atop Old Cock Rock, a portion of Hens and Chickens, where she sits this very day.

This rockpile has always been a double edged sword, providing some of the best fishing while waiting to claim any boat which ventured too close to her treacherous boulders. This location is prime ground for tautog, scup, sea bass, blues and trophy striped bass which utilize the cover and forage. Here is one spot where you can catch blackfish in excess of 10 pounds in the heat of August.

The wreck can be fished in moderate sized boats from nearby Westport Harbor or South Dartmouth. The southwest corner provides excellent topwater casting for blues feeding on the baitfish trapped in the tumult of waves. On the backside of the wreck scup, sea bass and tautog are taken on the shoulders of any rocky spikes which show up on your recorder. Every season, trophy bass are regularly taken off the northeast corner of the rockpile by sharpies using live eels or pogies, a baitfish found in the immediate area all summer long.

Don't get in too close and make sure your engine is finely tuned and your ground tackle heavy enough with plenty of scope to hold you fast. You don't want to be anywhere near this rockpile in nasty weather or breaking seas.

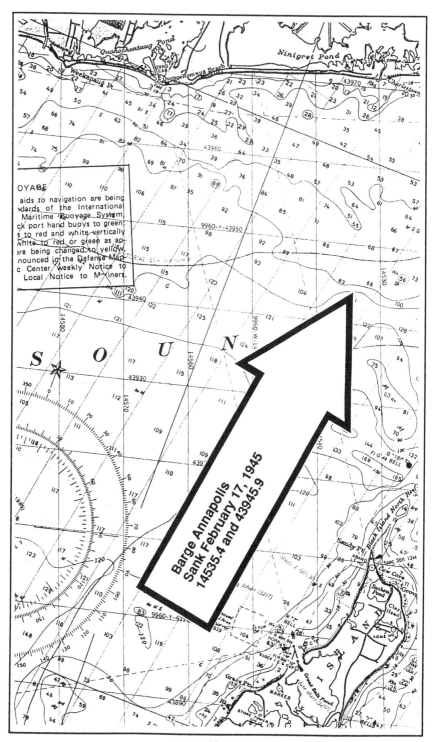

Barge Annapolis
Sank February 17, 1945
14535.4 and 43945.9

OYAGE
aids to navigation are being
dards of the International
Maritime Buoyage System,
ck port hand buoys to green,
s to red and white vertically
white to red or green as ap
are being changed to yellow.
nounced in the Defense Map
c Center weekly Notice to
Local Notice to Mariners.

S O U N

CHAPTER 3

Annapolis

This wooden coal barge came to her end on February 17, 1945 after colliding with a submarine coming into Block Island Sound. The sub was bound for the base at New London, Ct. In releasing news of the collision Third Naval District Headquarters said three men were tossed from the barge and picked up by the sub then taken to New London for care and observation. Luckily no one was hurt in this New England sea disaster. The day after the collision, a captain of a dragger from the nearby port of Stonington, Ct. found a lifeboat, preservers and other debris floating off Charlestown, R.I.

This 228 foot wreck is often nicknamed the Black Diamond because a diver's lights would reflect back from her coal cargo, giving the look of precious stones. At one point the bow of this large wreck rose 25 feet off the bottom but time and the elements took their toll. Today that section has collapsed though there's still plenty of wreckage to show up on the average fish finder.

Some divers surmised this wreck to be that of the Amelia Periera, a craft sunk before World War II at a position approximately 4-3/4 miles northwest of Sandy Point Light on Block Island. However, research at the Mystic Seaport Library showed the Amelia, a wooden fishing schooner, built at the John James Shipyard in Essex, Ma., was only 88 feet long, far too small to be this wreck.

Sportfishermen can expect to catch blackfish in the spring and fall as well as scup (porgies) in the summer months. You might also try a few drifts in the area to see if jumbo fluke have taken up residence nearby. If it's too windy for a small boat to head to Block Island for cod or blues, try the Annapolis. If we ever get a good run of codfish again in Block Island Sound here's a site that will hold fish. For cod I would recommend drifting over the wreck a few times with bait rig baited with fresh sea clams to see if anyone is home before anchoring. If you do get a few hits, then put your boat atop 14535.4 and 43945.9. Look for cod in Block Island Sound anytime after Thanksgiving, after the water cools down.

Like a lot of New England wrecks this one is not marked on current charts though it's well known to dragger captains from Point Judith and a few hook and line fishermen who've caught some nice blackfish. Probably the best bait for larger tautog is half of a green crab. Cut the crab down the middle, run a hook through one of the leg sockets then drop down to await results. One of the benefits of using crabs is you aren't normally bothered with small fish such as cunners.

As with wreckfishing overall fishermen can expect to lose rigging here. There's nets on the stern section plus debris lying all around the bottom. If you feel your line fast to something, don't yank on it. Instead give some slack line then whip the rod tip up and back several times. This will sometimes dislodge a hook. All hard steady pulling usually accomplishes is to drive the hook deeper into the snag, insuring a lost rig.

The steamer Aransas was sunk outside the entrance to Pollack Rip Channel on May 6, 1905. Photo courtesy of the Steamship Historical Society, University of Baltimore, Md.

CHAPTER 4

Aransas

On the evening of May 6, 1905 the 241 foot steamer Aransas left Boston bound for her regular run to New York. By 1 a.m. she had rounded the elbow of Cape Cod and was about to enter the narrow confines of a fog-shrouded Pollock Rip Channel, graveyard to many ships.

The officer in charge of Aransas rang down to the engine room to reduce speed. As he did he noticed the lights of a tug, the Patience, coming across his bow heading into the channel also. The tug blew its whistle indicating it should pass first with its barges. After two barges passed the whistle blowing stopped so the Aransas increased speed to make headway into the channel. Just as she did, a third barge appeared out of the fog to strike the steamer a death blow on her port bow.

Thanks to the discipline of captain and crew only one passenger lost her life in the collision. The Aransas settled by the bow; by the time the captain and last of the crew left the ship her decks were just about awash. Twenty or so minutes after the crash the Aransas slipped from sight.

The captain of the tug cast off his barges and went back to pick up the people from the Aransas. In time they were taken to Vineyard Haven and from there made their way to Providence, R.I. where most of them took another steamer to finish their trip. A couple days after the sinking, divers determined the ship a total loss, thus fair game for the wreckers' dynamite. She, like a lot of vessels before her, was blown up to prevent her from becoming a menace to navigation.

Today we find some of the remains of the Aransas at loran numbers 13837.0 and 43909.1. She's in 50 feet of water roughly southeast of Chatham, a prime spot for early spring or late fall codfishing in a small boat. I'll bet she holds codfish in season, perhaps into the summer, if water temperatures are on the cool side. Divers told me they've seen keeper codfish on the wreck of the Horatio Hall, not far away, right up through the Fourth of July.

In the early spring, some small boat anglers try to rush the season to end up heading out into weather they have no business in. Over the last ten years there's been a couple anglers and their rigs who've come to grief by not using some caution when the wind bucks against the tide. Even though you will not be far offshore on the Aransas, no amount of small cod is worth a dunking in a March ocean.

Another species you might encounter out there would be tautog. Some big ones hang their hats on the Hall, so an enterprising fisherman might check out this wreck for blackfish, too. If bait gathers above the wreck then bluefish will make a dinner stop here. If choppers are suspended above the wreck a diamond jig dropped to the bottom then speedily reeled to the top will catch them. If they're on the bottom then a chunk of fresh pogy (bunker) might be just the thing to get their interest and fill your fish box. You'll probably have to use weight to get it down in a running tide but results might be worth it.

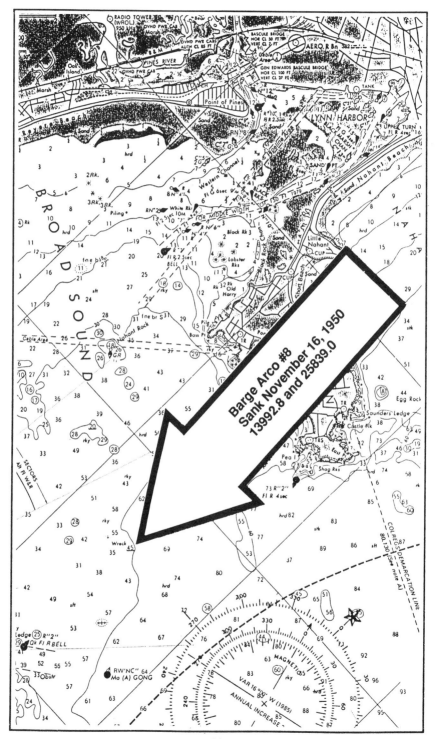

Barge Arco #8
Sank November 16, 1950
13992.8 and 25839.0

CHAPTER 5

Arco #8

There have been so many barge wrecks in New England over the years that some of those sinkings went unnoticed. Such seemed to be the case of the barge Arco #8 which sank east of Winthrop, Ma., on November 16, 1950.

We checked through back copies of the Boston Globe and Herald plus the Lynn Item but didn't find even one inch of space devoted to the event. Marine historian Mr. William Quinn of Orleans, Ma., suggested a publication called the Boston Marine Guide. We found their back copies had been destroyed in a fire so that, too, was a dead end. We finally hit "paydirt" with master wreck hunter Brad Luther of Fairhaven, Ma. Brad had a few scraps of information from old files of the Corps of Engineers.

The Arco #8 was 130 feet long with a 31 foot beam. She was on her way from Gloucester to Boston with a cargo of fish oil when she sank in Broad Sound from undetermined causes. Her position was given as 42-23-24 and 70-55-10 or 5,360 yards, 304 degrees from Graves Light. The best way to locate the wreck would be to head for loran numbers 13992.8 and 25839.0. If you eyeball those numbers on a current chart, you'll see a wreck symbol with 45 feet clearance, our target for this chapter.

Divers told us she sits upright on the bottom though parts are broken up. From their point of view, this is an uninteresting wreck though fishermen will take note because she'll hold codfish in the spring months. Here's another site close to the City of Salisbury, Sweet Sue or Romance, other wrecks listed in this book that are close by. All these "reefs" can be fished on an April day when the weather allows travel outside Boston Harbor. Just remember to throw the little guys back so there will be some next year.

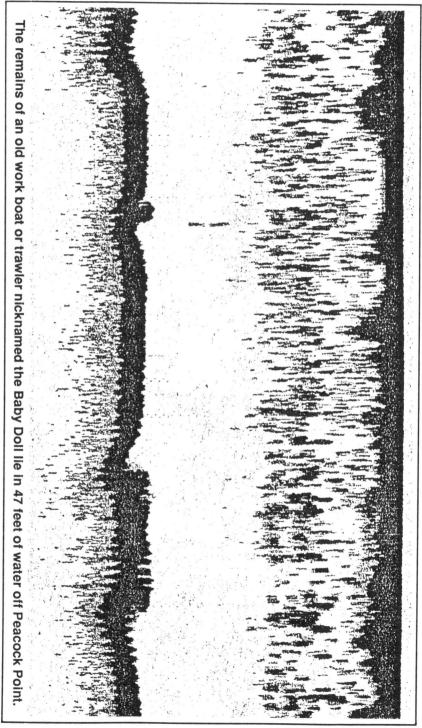

The remains of an old work boat or trawler nicknamed the Baby Doll lie in 47 feet of water off Peacock Point.

CHAPTER 6

Baby Doll

The earliest notice of this wreck we found was back in the 1930s. A Notice to Mariners in 1931 contained an item about the vessels Marindin and Ogden that would be doing a bottom survey in the vicinity of Great Captain Island off the coast of western Connecticut. From that point they would work their way eastward on wreck locations in the Sound.

This particular wreck was located in 47 feet of water on a soft mud bottom with clearance over it of 31 feet. It was and is located north of Peacock Point on the North Shore of Long Island. Over the years many divers and a few rod and reel fishermen located this structure either with land ranges or nowadays with a compact, inexpensive loran unit.

None of our sources for wreck information in this area knew the identity of this one. Diver Stan Schwartz and his friend Ed Koystra nicknamed the ship Baby Doll because on their first dive here they found a baby's doll among other items.

Stan said the ship looks to be either a tug or fishing dragger since there are winches on the deck. The housing is gone and she's split into two pieces so maybe it was the victim of a collision. The vessel was guesstimated to be 80 to 90 feet long with each section about 30 to 40 feet. In between the sections there's a 25 foot gap. What's left of the Baby Doll comes up around 7 feet at its highest point so you'll be able to spot it on a chart recorder.

The Baby Doll, at 26880.3 and 43954.8, is within easy range of people who keep their boats on the western end of Long Island Sound. Stan has seen nice flounders in the soft bottom close to the wreckage as well as blackfish. For you divers, he's noted he's pulled some nice lobsters off it too.

The bow of the Baby Doll lies to 30 degrees while the stern section is oriented 270 degrees. We'll bet a green crab or nice, juicy sand worm would arouse attention if dropped down. If there's no action on the bottom you can easily run to any of the other wrecks in this area mentioned in the book or you might switch to blues.

For blues we'd recommend a nice, fresh piece of cut bunker fished down on the botton, or, if you mark bait hanging above the wreck, break out the wire line outfits and the umbrella rigs. Troll back and forth in the area, keeping the rig as far down in the water as you can.

Since wire line goes down 10 feet (roughly) for every 100 feet of wire out, you'll need a heap of wire line to get down this far. What you might do is put out 300 feet and make sure all the wire is in the water then turn the boat right or left when you get over the wreck. This will drop the rod on the inside of the turn down lower. The sharper the turn, the deeper the rig will go. Don't let it fall too far or you'll hook the wreck, not what's hanging over it. If you do lose an expensive umbrella rig your next move might be to befriend a diver.

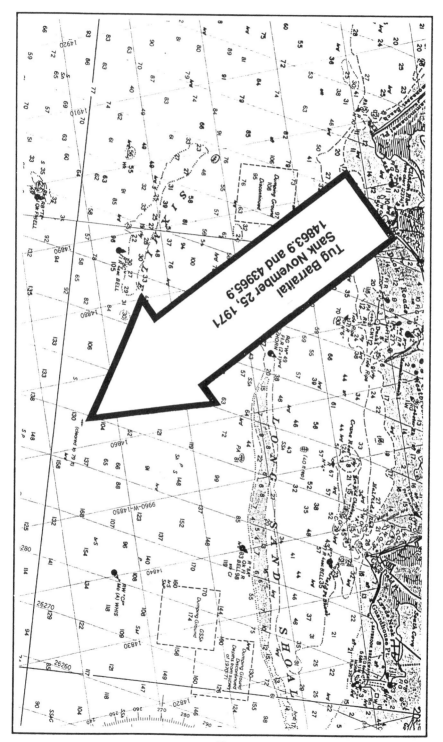

Tug Barratal
Sank November 25, 1971
14863.9 and 43965.9

CHAPTER 7

Barraitai

On November 25, 1971 a fierce northeaster slammed into New England. Twenty inches of snow were reported in some sections along with plenty of snarled Thanksgiving traffic. Boston had 2-1/2 inches of rain and gale winds but Montpelier, Vt., had 18 inches of snow. There were fender benders galore and numerous sections were without power.

While the storm caused a lot of people aggravation and inconvenience, a far more threatening aspect of the blow took place in the eastern section of Long Island Sound. The tugboat Barraitai left Middletown, Ct., on the day of the storm bound for Coral Gables, Fl., to engage in a salvage operation. Once out in the Sound the high, choppy seas from the winds caused the tug to take on water, knocking out the power supply and with that went the pumps.

As the tug's predicament became worse, a couple flares were shot off. One was seen by police at Southold over on Long Island while the other was spotted by a woman who phoned the information to the Coast Guard. A cutter was dispatched from New London, Ct., and a helicopter from Brooklyn, N.Y. Upon arriving they found three survivors clinging to an oil drum. One man died from exposure, a fourth crewman was never found.

Today the tug sits at 14863.9 and 43965.9 in 135 to 140 feet of water; she's deep for diving and for a lot of the sportfishing done in Long Island Sound.

I often thought an enterprising fisherman or woman could find a tautog fishery right through the summer in the Sound by fishing some of the deeper wrecks in this book. Right now blackfishing usually ends in early summer and doesn't really get started again until the water cools in the fall. Perhaps on some of these deeper spots a person might find worthwhile fishing right through the heat of August.

Some anglers told me in the past it wasn't possible to catch tautog during the height of a full moon tide because you couldn't hold bottom. Well, one day Mr. Phil Wetmore and I went out with wire line and 44 ounces of lead to catch an Igloo cooler full of tautog right through the strength of a roaring tide. Someone might need to do the same on some days on these deeper wrecks. Such fishing will not be to everyone's tastes but it is possible.

Mr. Sherwood Lincoln of River's End Tackle Shop in Old Saybrook, Ct. told me about a couple fishermen who drift fished the deep water in the middle of the Sound with heavy sinkers and wire line. They caught some jumbo sea bass and larger scup, further fueling the thought there's deep-water fishing in the Sound going uninvestigated.

The bottom around the tug is peaky so you might wander around a bit taking loran readings on the top of some of the hills then drift over them with a drail rig baited with herring or try speed squidding with heavier jigs hoping for fish at mid-depth. This deep water fishing might not be your cup of tea but the possibilities are there.

-19-

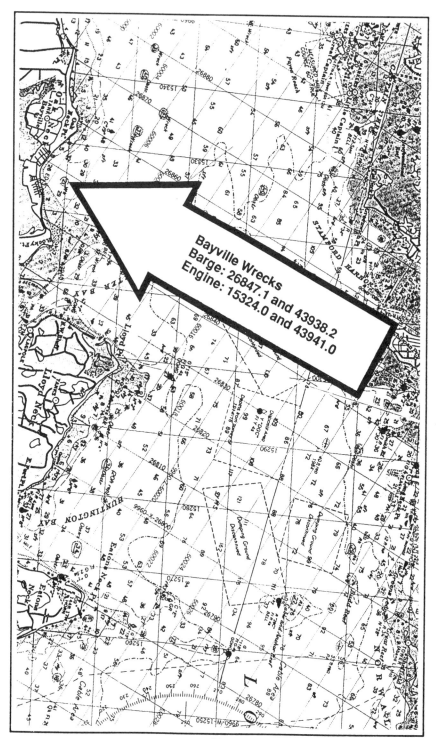

Bayville Wrecks
Barge: 26847.1 and 43938.2
Engine: 15324.0 and 43941.0

-20-

CHAPTER 8

Bayville Wrecks

Sometime after World War I some obsolete ships were sunk outside Bayville, Long Island, N.Y. to form a breakwater to protect a dock for the upcoming ferry service from there to Greenwich, Ct. All or some of the ships used were U.S. Navy subs.

According to Ms. Gladys Mack, historian for the village of Bayville, the ferry service started running in 1921 and ended service in November, 1937. Afterwards the Bayville Board of Trustees declared the ships a hazard and some of them were towed away.

In a February 9, 1943 issue of The New York Times there was a three inch news item about the Nassau County War Council Salvage Committee looking into plans to salvage four submarines that were part of the ferry breakwater to aid the WWII effort. The article stated the submarines had been looked over and were worth raising for scrap.

The site of the scuttlings was opposite Rheinhard's Restaurant, now the Walls Beach Restaurant. In September of 1988, Officer Richard Taracka of the Greenwich Police Marine Squad, in response to our inquiry, contacted a man named Jim, one of the sons of the original owners of Rheinhard's. Jim thought the wrecks had been sunk by filling the hulls with stones and he further remembers the date the subs were salvaged was August, 1943. It's likely some parts of the Bayville Subs, as the wreck site is nicknamed by divers, remains today.

In the summer of 1988 the NOAA research ship Heck, investigating wrecks in Long Island Sound, found the remains of an engine that rose 6 to 8 feet off a muddy bottom. The loran numbers are 15324.0 and 43941.0. Whether this is part of a sub or other ship is work to be done by some enterprising diver.

While checking out the background for this wreck we corresponded with Mr. Lada Simek, a diver from Ossining, N.Y. Lada knew of the background of the subs and he volunteered information that at 26847.1 and 43938.2 there is another wreck, completely broken up, of a barge. Perhaps it sank during the salvage or it's there from some unrelated mishap? Whatever the case it's another structure close by to provide cover and grounds for sportfishing.

We suspect one could find flounders in the soft bottom around both areas plus blackfish close to the wrecks themselves. If there's bait and cover you might just find some bass prowling for a meal. A 40 pound striper will not turn her nose up at a one pound flounder or blackfish. Some of the bass sharpies on Long Island have been livelining those two baits on the sly for many years. Such bass baits are not widely used in other areas of New England but they will work for the fisherman willing to take the time for trial and error.

If there's bait and cover on an otherwise flat bottom you stand a chance at catching bluefish from time to time. One might try casting over the wrecks with a plug some calm morning or evening for topwater excitement.

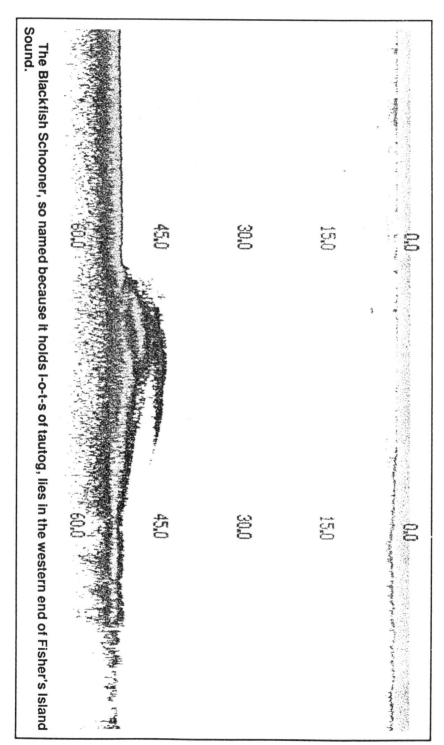

The Blackfish Schooner, so named because it holds l-o-t-s of tautog, lies in the western end of Fisher's Island Sound.

CHAPTER 9

Blackfish Schooner

This is one of the many unknown wrecks off our shores. Sitting in 50 feet of water not far from the western entrance of Fisher's Island Sound is the wreck of an old schooner. One experienced diver told us the ship has probably been there a lot of years. The fast tides flushing the Sound keep it from silting in like so many other old vessels.

The day we verified the numbers at 26116.5 and 43978.6 we found schools of blackfish hanging over the 100 foot wreck like a thin cloud. On pass after pass over the Blackfish Schooner we caught blackfish after blackfish, some to 6 pounds. I don't know how long we might have stayed but good sense and the need to hunt more wrecks kept our total to 40-plus blacks destined for a hot winter's chowder.

The Blackfish Schooner isn't far from the state launching ramp at Bayberry Lane in Groton, Ct., making it ideal for someone with a boat of limited means. If the weather during tautog season is too windy to venture outside you can sometimes hide behind Fisher's Island in relative comfort to catch a comfortable share of fish here. If the weather becomes a problem, you're only a short distance from safety. During the fall, when tautog season is at its peak, the ramp usually has plenty of elbow room, even on weekends. Don't expect the same room if you try the schooner during the summer for fluke. During those times you can wait up to an hour to get your boat back on the trailer when everyone decides to head for supper at the same time.

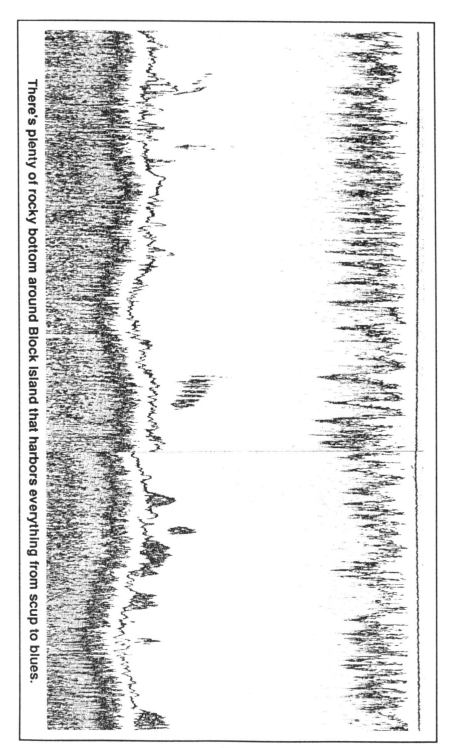

There's plenty of rocky bottom around Block Island that harbors everything from scup to blues.

CHAPTER 10

Block Island Numbers

During the two years of work that went into this book we researched quite a bit of underwater territory. Some days we found a bonafide shipwreck but on more trips than we like to think about we found rockpiles. While they certainly weren't our primary target they will indeed be places for ground or gamefish to feed. The following is a list of such places around Block Island with a short explanation of what you might expect to catch, depending on season. To what's below we might add that most rockpiles have the potential of bluefishing if bait gathers.

25874.9 and 43930.5 to 25875.6 and 43930.5
Big rockpile north of Block. Codfish in the spring, possibly scup in the summer. Tautog in spring and fall.

14523.6 and 43926.6
One lone, large rock north of the island. Could hold all of the above and maybe some fluke.

14585.0 and 43965.7
Leftover stone from building of Weekapaug Breachway dumped here. Cod, blackfish and scup.

14616.3 and 43962.1
Rockpile to the northwest of Block over to Watch Hill. Try for scup, fluke or tautog during summer months. Possible codfish in fall and winter.

14500.1 and 43948.3 to 14497.2 and 43950.9
Rock bottom north of Block off Matunuck. Groundfishing.

14552.8 to 53.2 and 43960.7 to 60.5
Peaky bottom in Block Island Sound off Quonochontaug. Groundfishing. Some stretches will eat sinkers.

14547.7 and 43864.8
Nicknamed the Pinnacle, south of the island. Cod are here in spring and fall. Sometimes large scup in late fall.

14640.2 and 43801.4
Rock bottom southwest of Block over toward Montauk. Known producer of cod, groundfish.

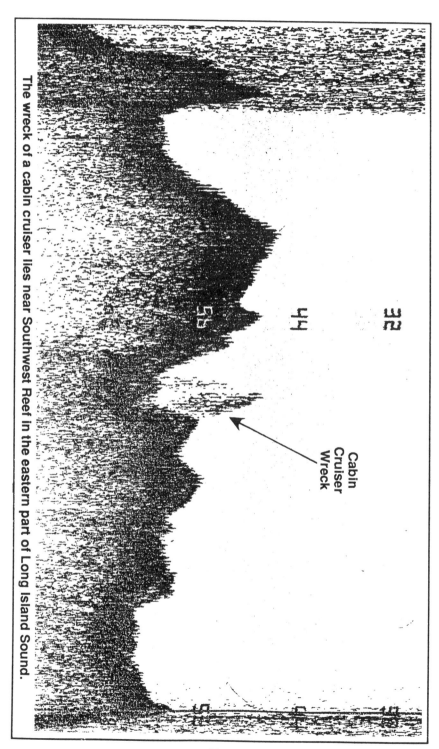

32

44

56

Cabin
Cruiser
Wreck

The wreck of a cabin cruiser lies near Southwest Reef in the eastern part of Long Island Sound.

CHAPTER 11

Cabin Cruiser

If you like to fish for scup this wreck is for you. Look on navigational charts for the eastern part of Long Island Sound. Roughly southeast of the end of the Kelsey Point Breakwater you'll see a wreck symbol. There lies a cabin cruiser sunk in May, 1973.

A notice in the weekly Notice to Mariners stated the 26 foot craft sunk in 45 feet of water about 2,550 yards from the breakwater. The time of the notice was the 25th week of that year.

This wreck was found by a commercial rod and reel fisherman scouting Southwest Reef for places that would provide a good load of scup (porgies) on a daily basis. He stumbled across this small wreck but kept it quiet for many years until we teamed up to locate other areas in the Sound. During one such wreck hunt he volunteered the information you are reading.

The small wreck sits on the western side of a hump near Southwest Reef, a known producer of tautog, scup, bluefish and lobsters. On many, many trips this commercial fisherman made his day's pay with 100 to 200 pound catches of scup at this location. We'd guess the same wreck would be worth a drop for blackfish once the weather cools down in the fall. Southwest Reef area is a candidate as one of the best blackfishing spots on the Connecticut shore.

To fish this wreck head out for 26352.2 and 43995.6. You may have to look around as this isn't a big target. If your fish finder has the ability to expand a section of the bottom, such a feature would come in handy here. All around the wreck are reefs which go up and down like a mini roller coaster; the wreck will appear as a somewhat "hollow" rockpile.

The commercial man would anchor his 20 foot center console bass boat directly atop the structure then proceed to use a light rod with sensitive tip. He'd bait up a hi-lo, two hook rig with pieces of fresh squid gotten from a local dragger captain. If the tide wasn't running hard he'd also use a chumpot to hold fish where he wanted them.

Scup fishing isn't the shoo-in some anglers think it is. Scup are notorious bait stealers that require a deft hand on a light rod to land them consistently. If you wait too long in a scup's bite you'll spend the day rebaiting. One trick you might try, if the day isn't going well, is to slowly raise the rig a foot or so off bottom then very slowly lower it back down. This causes the small pieces of squid to flutter a bit in the current, sometimes provoking more bites than a rig just sitting on the bottom.

Charley Soares with a small cod he jigged up on a hill off Manomet Point, north of the Mars wreck.

Cape Cod Bay Numbers

Besides having its share of shipwrecks, Cape Cod Bay also sports a large section of rocky bottom which is ideal for groundfishing in a smaller boat since most of it is within easy range of shore. Most of the catch is liable to be cod though there's the chance at some tautog. We do know there's an ongoing tautog fishery off the Gurnet so we don't see why other rocky stretches close by might not have some blackfish on them. One charter captain from Green Harbor is so sure of a tautog fishery along the south shore he started offering trips for them this fall.

13894.0 X 44074.0
Fishing Ledge, center of the bay. Codfishing in season and some flounders. Gillnetters have these numbers too.

13957.5 X 44095.7
Hill off Manomet Point, north of Mars wreck. Groundfish, possible blues.

13973.7 X 44129.1
Rocky bottom off Gurnet Point.

13972.3 X 44127.8
Same as above. Lobster pots in area.

13967.7 X 44130.4
More groundfishing off the Gurnet.

13928.7 X 44174.6
Rockpile coming up 8 feet near Pinthis wreck.

13929.6 X 44174.7
Smaller rockpile, also near Pinthis.

The concrete freighter Cape Fear was sunk in a collision in the East Passage of Narragansett Bay on October 29, 1920. Photo courtesy of the Mariners Museum.

CHAPTER 13

Cape Fear

The career of the concrete freighter Cape Fear was a short one. She was built in 1919 at the Liberty Shipbuilding Company in Wilmington, N.C. On October 29, 1920 she went to the bottom of the East Passage of Narragansett Bay in 160 feet of water.

Born out of the steel shortages of World War I the concrete shipbuilding program ended a failure. Twelve large concrete ships were built, a lot of which ended up on the floor of the ocean. In all, the Cape Fear carried only two cargoes before her sinking after a collision with the steamer City of Atlanta.

After a scheduling mixup which sent two crews to man her for the same voyage, the Cape Fear departed Providence, R.I. Her destination was to be the James River in Virginia where she would join other idle vessels. Her captain decided to drop off his harbor pilot prematurely and proceeded under his direction down the passage of the bay. As his ship and the City of Atlanta approached each other they exchanged whistle signals indicating who would pass to what side. Each ship acknowledged each other's signals but for some reason the Cape Fear pulled across the bow of the oncoming ship. The much larger Atlanta crashed into the Cape Fear almost cutting her in two. She sank in three minutes with a loss of 17 lives. The City of Atlanta's seamen rescued survivors then the ship steamed the next morning to Providence for unloading and damage inspection. An inquiry by the United States Steamboat Inspection Service found the captain of the Cape Fear guilty of three counts of negligence for which he lost his license as Master of Coastal Vessels.

At 266 feet long with a 46 foot beam the Cape Fear is one of the larger inshore wrecks. You'll find her at 14394.7 and 43993.5, right in a high traffic area, particularly during the busy summer months. If you plan to fish this spot during a Sunday sailboat race we suggest another wreck.

At times anglers could drift across this wreck and try speed squidding for blues or perhaps drop a bait rig down baited with whole or chunk pogy. If you're new to speed squidding, the method is to take a diamond jig, usually six ounces, drop it to bottom of the wreck then reel as fast as you can until the lure is about a third of the way back. If there's no hits, drop the jig again and keep repeating until you drift away from the wreck or there's too much line out for effective hook setting.

Back in the days of better codfishing some fishermen used to catch baccala right in the deep water of this passage. If our groundfish populations rebound to the point we can have fishing close to the Rhode Island coast I'd make it a point to head for the Cape Fear.

The tugboat Celtic sank off the Norwalk Islands on November 17, 1984. Photo courtesy of Steve Cryan Studios.

CHAPTER 14

Celtic

On November 17, 1984 the 85 foot tugboat Celtic along with a 140 foot barge loaded with scrap iron, the Cape Race, left Bridgeport, Ct., bound for Port Newark, N.J. The time was 8:00 p.m. During that night the mate on the tug contacted the dispatcher at the home office saying he would be off Execution Light sometime around 2:00 a.m. He also radioed other vessels in the area requesting information on sea conditions. Those were the last messages anyone ever heard from the doomed Celtic.

The next day the tug's owner got in touch with the Coast Guard to report the vessel overdue. On the 19th, divers located the tug in approximately 68 feet of water at 41-01.8 and 73-24.6. Along with the discovery came the recovery of what was to be six bodies; no one survived the sinking. On the 21st the barge was located a short distance from the tug.

A Coast Guard investigation and report on the mishap noted the tug was pushing the barge when she departed Bridgeport. Sometime during the night we can surmise the captain decided to change the tow so the barge was lashed to the tug's starboard side, perhaps after the crewman radioed other vessels for the sea conditions which were moderate at the time.

The barge was in bad shape having sustained damage through previous voyages that went unrepaired. Prior to the sinking, a maintenance man said he'd pumped out the barge after finding it taking on water. It was assumed the barge opened up during the tow and filled with water so rapidly she took the tug and six men down with her before an alarm could be sounded. Divers found no evidence of anything other than poor souls overcome so quickly they did not know what hit them.

Located off the fishy Norwalk Islands at 26798.7 and 43989.6, the wrecks provide ample blackfishing which will likely increase as time and marine growth accelerate the process of underwater deterioration. I imagine the wrecks will be the spot for some really jumbo blacks though heavy tackle is needed to get them up away from line-parting debris before the blackfish returns to his hole.

A simple blackfish rig can be made by tying a dropper loop about six inches up from another loop used to hold a sinker heavy enough to tend bottom. A six inch dropper on the top loop is fine. Completing the rig would be a number four Virginia-style hook baited with half of a green crab. The less hardware one uses while blackfishing, especially around wrecks, the less likely the chances of snagging. If you do get hung up, you will not lose much in the way of terminal gear.

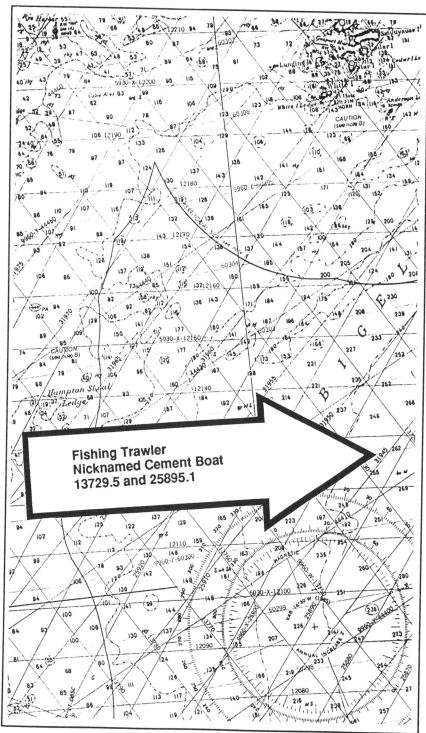

Fishing Trawler
Nicknamed Cement Boat
13729.5 and 25895.1

CHAPTER 15

Cement Boat

For this next wreck we relied on local fishermen's knowledge as she's too deep for scuba divers to investigate. Some fishermen surmised the wreck we located in October, 1988 with the help of Captain Ron Ward on the charter boat Family Affair, was a cement barge bound for Portland, Maine. However, the target on the color fish finder looked way too small to be a barge.

Further checking along the waterfront in Newburyport, Ma., revealed the probable name of this small wreck to be the Fero Queen, a cement fishing boat built in a shed on land now occupied by the Windward Yacht Club on the Merrimack River.

To build this 40 footer a shed needed high humidity so it could be filled with steam to enable each layer of cement to be trawled in place. Upon completion the boat was either coming or going past the Isle of Shoals when she struck something in the water. The collision opened up her seams and eventually her crew lost the fight to save her. She sank in about 240 feet of water where she remains today. The housing on her was wood which was eventually torn off by other draggers.

Most people along the water were reluctant to have their names mentioned as it seems a hard hat diver went down on the wreck for salvage but unfortunately lost his life in the attempt. As you might expect, such wounds never quite heal so we honored those requests for anonymity. One local fishing captain did say our loran numbers looked correct though he only had old loran A readings.

The cement boat wreck is within easy range of the mouth of the Merrimack. I'll bet she holds codfish attracted as they are to wrecks in various locations around New England. Fishermen might be able to drift across the spot with jigs and tubes. Normally such jigging on wrecks is an invitation to disaster in lost gear but the cement boat may be one of those wrecks you can fish without too many lost jigs. If you want to be on the safe side try a couple passes with a bait rig baited with fresh sea clams. If there's any market cod at home I'll bet you get their immediate attention.

If you get some hits you could obviously keep drifting or anchor up if you have the expertise to do so. Putting say a 25 foot center console atop something only 40 feet long in 40 plus fathoms will no doubt tax your seamanship and anchor line capacity.

You'll find this wreck at 13729.5 and 25895.1. If you're loking for a good teaser to try above your jig we'd recommend a Red Gill in the four or six inch size. The vibrating tail gets codfish to eat them with the same enthusiasm divers or fishermen seek wreck numbers.

During the spring, some of the inshore rockpiles might harbor a steaker or two like this 36 pounder.

CHAPTER 16

Chatham Rockpiles

This section is loran numbers of what we think are rockpiles, not wrecks, though none have been investigated by divers. One is close to the wreck symbol marked 60 feet clearance due east of Chatham while a few others are down to the east of the broken part of Pollock Rip.

The day we investigated these numbers three of them had bait just above the rocks and two showed orange blotches just above which indicated a school of codfish on a color fish finder. All these locations are close enough so if early spring weather threatened a man in a smaller boat he could make shore in time.

13788.4 to 13788.6 X 43919.5 to 43919.9
Rockpile north of the 60 wreck.

13789.9 to 13790.0 X 43915.5 to 43915.6
Rockpile close to 60 wreck.

13826.3 to 13826.6 X 43883.5 to 43883.9
Holds smaller codfish some tides.

13821.2. to 13821.4 X 43877.8 to 43878.2
Same as above.

13802.2 X 43914.1
Large rock west of 60 wreck.

The coastal tanker Chelsea was sunk off Gloucester on February 10, 1957. Photo courtesy of the Peabody Museum of Salem, Ma.

CHAPTER 17

Chelsea

While reduced populations of cod along sections of the southern New England coast mean there's not much of an inshore fishery any more, sections of the North Shore of Massachusetts still enjoy fair to good cod catching in close. One of the spots is off the town of Gloucester, scene of many wrecks, including the coastal tanker Chelsea which sank on February 10, 1957.

The 175 foot Chelsea was proceeding up the coast from Boston bound for Newington, N.H. The ship was hugging the coast trying to get in the lee of a 35 mph "breeze." About midday the skipper turned the ship over to the chief mate so he could go below. One half hour later he felt a bump and went topside to investigate. He found his ship hard aground on Avery Ledge, the sunken section on the southern end of the Rockport Breakwater. Fishing boats often duck between Straitsmouth Island and the breakwater to shorten their trip only they make sure to give the ledge adequate clearance.

The crew of the tanker was taken off and brought to a nearby Coast Guard Station. An inspection revealed an 80 foot gash in the tanker's hull from bow to amidships. Coast Guard personnel decided it might be worth a try to repair the ship while she was aground so the crew and captain were brought back. Unfortunately the incoming tide floated the damaged ship free around 6 p.m. As soon as that happened a nearby 36 foot motorized lifeboat came over and took most of the crew off then took a hawser from the Chelsea to run it out to a cutter to attempt a tow.

The captain of the Chelsea started the engines in a futile attempt to save her but high winds pushed her south and she started to take on water. By the time she was opposite Loblolly Cove she was settling rapidly by the bow. The man in charge of the lifeboat ran his craft right alongside the tanker to get the rest of the crew off. As the tanker sank, other Coast Guardsmen axed the hawser to keep their craft from being pulled under. The Chelsea sank into roughly 60 feet of 37 degree water.

Today the remains of the Chelsea can be found at 13777.6 and 25797.5. Most of the hull is broken up and flattened on the bottom though the bow is intact. She's close to shore for the man in a small boat to enjoy codfishing. If there's no action on the wreck an angler might head off to the south a short distance where there are numerous rockpiles and ledges off both the Manchester and Salem shores.

We suspect most of the cod you'll catch in these areas will be smaller ones. A 15 pounder would be a nice catch but we think you'll fish hard before you catch a steaker.

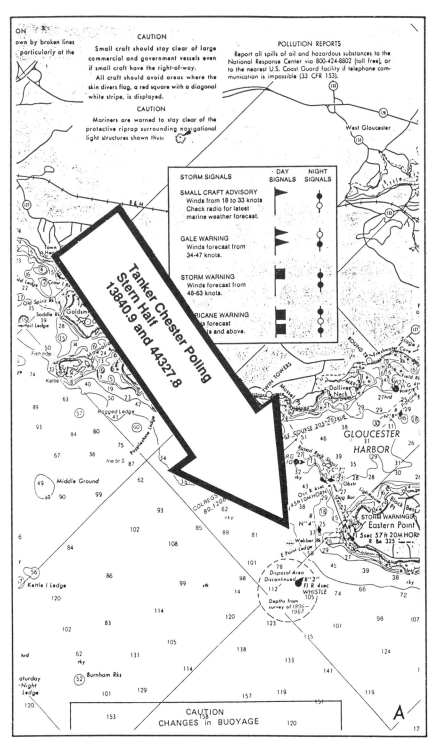

ON
own by broken lines
particularly at the

CAUTION

Small craft should stay clear of large commercial and government vessels even if small craft have the right-of-way.

All craft should avoid areas where the skin divers flag, a red square with a diagonal white stripe, is displayed.

CAUTION

Mariners are warned to stay clear of the protective riprap surrounding navigational light structures shown thus:

POLLUTION REPORTS

Report all spills of oil and hazardous substances to the National Response Center via 800-424-8802 (toll free), or to the nearest U.S. Coast Guard facility if telephone communication is impossible (33 CFR 153).

West Gloucester

Tanker Chester Poling
Stern Half
13840.9 and 44327.8

STORM SIGNALS	DAY SIGNALS	NIGHT SIGNALS
SMALL CRAFT ADVISORY Winds from 18 to 33 knots Check radio for latest marine weather forecast.		
GALE WARNING Winds forecast from 34-47 knots.		
STORM WARNING Winds forecast from 48-63 knots.		
HURRICANE WARNING Winds forecast ...ts and above.		

GLOUCESTER HARBOR

COLREGS 80.1200

Middle Ground

Ragged Ledge

Poplahoons Ledge

Kettle I Ledge

Burnham Rks

Saturday Night Ledge

STORM WARNINGS
Eastern Point
5 sec 57 ft 20 M HORN
R Bn 325

Disposal Area
Discontinued

R "2"
Fl R 4 sec
WHISTLE

Depths from survey of 1896—1967

CAUTION
CHANGES in BUOYAGE

A

-40-

CHAPTER 18

Chester Poling

We only have half of a wreck for you in this section. The stern half of the Chester Poling broke apart and sank along with the bow off Gloucester, Ma., on January 11, 1977. As of press time, we understand the bow section was located in 1989 with the aid of a Klein Side Scan Sonar device. She's in 185 feet of water, laying upside down on the bottom. We do not have the numbers of that half so we'll turn our attention to the stern and details of the sinking.

The 281 foot Chester Poling, an aging coastal tanker, was making her way from Boston up to Newington, N.H. Thank goodness she was empty or her normal capacity of 840,000 gallons would have fouled area beaches. About 10:30 that morning the captain of the Poling sent out an urgent message that the ship was breaking up in 50 knot winds and 20 foot seas. Seconds later another message was received at the Coast Guard Station at Harbor Loop that the ship had broken apart.

As the first Coast Guard vessels arrived on the scene they tried in vain to get a line on the halves but were unable to do so because of the horrendous sea conditions. One young Coast Guardsman sustained a back injury through a fall on deck so that ship started for home. At that point the bow section couldn't take any more and started to go down. Terrible sea conditions or not, with the men from the bow thrown in the 40 degree water, one Coast Guard boat closed in. The captain was taken in on the first pass but it took another 15 minutes of tricky maneuvering to get into position to pick up the second man.

As that rescue was taking place, other Coast Guard boats circled the stern. A helicopter was ordered from Buzzards Bay but was unable to lift off right away because of the lousy weather. Eventually they got clearance and arrived on the scene just after the bow sank. The pilot of the copter hovered over the stern to get one man off in a rescue basket. A second seaman made a jump for his life but missed the basket to land in the icy water. His body was never recovered. At that point the stern couldn't take any more buffeting from the seas; it too started to sink, throwing the remaining crew members in the frigid Atlantic. Coast Guard boats immediately closed in to rescue the last men from certain death from hypothermia. In all, only one man was lost, thanks to another life-over-death rescue by the U.S. Coast Guard.

The stern of the Poling can be found at 13840.9 and 44327.8. Divers say she's loaded with small cod at times but be advised the Poling is a very popular dive spot so you may not be able to fish it when you want. If there's a dive boat there, go seek some of the other places close by.

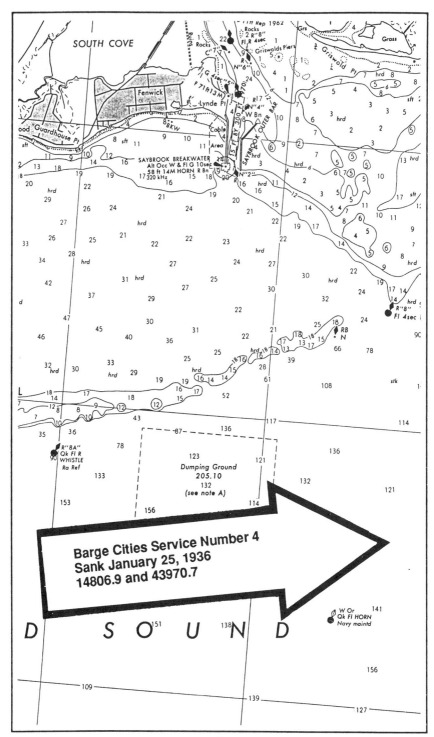

Barge Cities Service Number 4
Sank January 25, 1936
14806.9 and 43970.7

CHAPTER 19

Cities Service Number 4

The headline in a shoreline Connecticut newspaper read an oil barge sank the day before in Long Island Sound and two men were in a hospital suffering from exposure. The date was January 25, 1936.

Some 43 years after the sinking, anglers can jig blues on some trips over top of what is now a man-made reef that sticks up off the bottom 15 feet in 143 feet of water. Here's how the Cities Service Number Four barge came to her final rest.

She was being towed up the Sound after leaving Bayway, N.J., bound for Braintree, Ma. Off Faulkner's Island, in heavy west winds and seas, the water swept over the barge time and time again, knocking out windows in the deck cabin and flooding the cabin to a depth of four feet. A short time later the mate on the barge climbed atop the mast to signal the captain of the tug Dauntless which was towing the barge that his craft was going down.

The captain turned the Dauntless around to head back to render assistance. The barge mate and captain had by then climbed a pipe high over the deck to keep from being swept overboard. Several attempts to get a line to the two men failed until, finally, a fifth try hit home. The captain tied the line around the mate's waist as his hands were frozen. He threw the mate overboard so people on the tug could pull him in. The captain fastened the rope around himself then he, too, took the necessary plunge into the icy water to save his life. Cities Service Number Four sank at roughly 1:30 p.m. The cause of the sinking was likely one or more of her seams opened up in the heavy seas.

The barge now sits at 14806.9 and 43970.7 in deep water to be sure but you can locate the wreck then run uptide a bit to drop a diamond jig to bottom then speedily squid it a third of the way back to you. If there's no hits, repeat the squidding until you've drifted away from the wreck. Don't waste time fishing away from the wreck which holds the bait which holds the blues unless you mark fish on your machine. Bluefish might not be around each and every day but this spot is worth a stop, especially in the fall when fish are schooling. If the tide is running too hard, try returning toward the end when it's easy to reach bottom with a four to six inch jig.

One addition to a jig usually welcomed by bluefish is a surge tube on the back. The best colors are red, white and green though any color of the rainbow sees use. If you're fishing with lighter line, tie a piece of 50 to 80 pound line between your fishing line and the jig. That way you can reach down and grab hold of the leader to swing medium fish aboard if your partner is busy with the gaff.

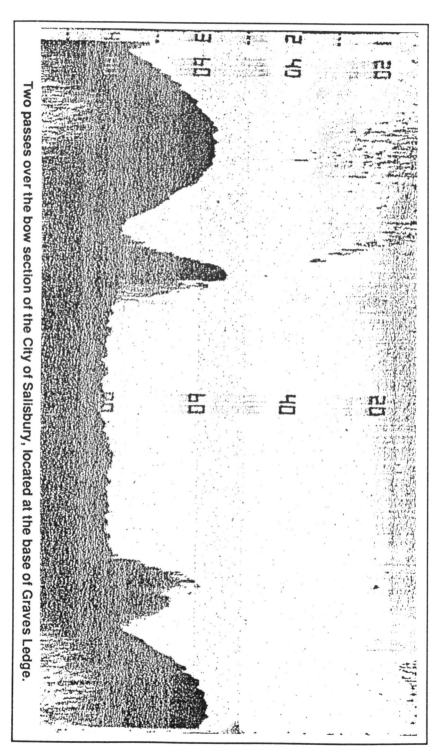

Two passes over the bow section of the City of Salisbury, located at the base of Graves Ledge.

CHAPTER 20

City of Salisbury

This wreck got the nicknames of Zoo or Jungle Ship because she carried, among other cargo, animals from Calcutta, India, bound for an importer in New York. However, the 419 foot ship made a stop in Boston; that stop turned out to be the end of the line.

On April 22, 1938, the ship hit the pinnacle rock at Graves Ledge just outside Boston Harbor. At first the ship was in no immediate danger but eventually the motion of the seas broke her apart just forward of her stack. The bow fell down into 80 feet of water where the remains of it remain today.

All the crew and animals were removed though some of the poor creatures died from exposure due to the dampness of a pier in East Boston in April. After the ship broke apart, her cargo spilled out of her hold and onto nearby Nantasket Beach. More than 100 cartons of tea, 105 pounds to the carton, were recovered on shore. All the local citizenry developed a new-found interest in beachcombing as word of the shipwreck spread around town.

Luckily no one was killed in this wreck. After the ship split, a tugboat pulled up to the stern to take all the remaining crew members off. Some salvage was carried out before the stern section too slipped under. Today there's scattered wreckage on both sides of the ledge.

Divers tell us the bow section is at 13974.4 and 44283.3. All that's left today is broken and scattered plates which leads one to believe both halves were dynamited to keep other ships from striking them. However, there's plenty of bow wreckage left to show up on the average fish finder. If you look on current charts you'll see a wreck marked off right atop the ledge but such isn't the case any more. The bow sits on the bottom at approximately the base of the ledge.

Anyone who follows the fishing in Boston Harbor knows the school codfishing can be fair to excellent depending on weather and location. We'll bet the wreck of the City of Salisbury will hold small cod. It's in a location where someone in a small boat could get to it on decent weather days. We also imagine a rig baited with clams might be better than jigging since wrecks with all the jagged debris have a tendency to eat cod jigs for breakfast.

During the summer months one might find some blues prowling this area. Most wrecks hold bait which is what bluefish like for supper.

A lot of the wrecks in western Long Island Sound will produce nice blackfish.

[""]

Coal Barge

Situated in the western end of Long Island Sound this is but one of the many barges sunk there during the last 100 years. Think of all the traffic that comes and goes to the port of New York. For almost every year of that time span there's been a wreck in the Sound from Norwalk down to Execution Light.

Some of those wrecks are now no more than a muddy pile of debris while others still present a striking bottom profile. Still others are in various stages of destruction depending on the length of time they've been buried under so many feet of green or brown Sound water.

One of the many unknown wrecks in this region, this coal barge was found by diver Lada Simek of Ossining, N.Y. He said it's pretty well broken up though there's still some machinery recognizable on deck. Its coal cargo is plainly visible to anyone who would care to dive on yet another barge wreck.

This barge is about 150 feet long with a 40 or so foot beam. She'll only show about a 3 to 4 foot rise on a fish finder but that doesn't mean it will not hold fish. Some of the best fishing wrecks are those that have tumbled down around themselves providing cover and growth for baitfish and species like blackfish. Once a wreck has been on the bottom a few years it attracts marine growth. Once that starts, crabs and small baitfish home in on the structure seeking relief from those that would eat them. Once the crabs and bait gather, the tautog are not far behind.

Not only will a wreck provide food for the blackfish it also offers them a home. As long as the blackfish is happy where he or she is it'll stay put until it's time for a seasonal migration. One blackfish attracts another and in time a whole school takes up residence. The angler who locates these places often has him or herself a fishing hotspot.

Once you do find a wreck, try not to fish it too hard or you'll keep the fish population from building back up. If, say, you and your partner took a catch of 40 tautog off a wreck, leave it alone for a bit until the fish population regroups. Prudent use of a wreck means it will have good fishing when your next day off rolls around.

This particular wreck can be located at 26930.5 and 43945.7. She's right in mid-Sound so it would be possible to fish the Long Island side then hit her on the way home if you keep a boat in Westchester County or the Connecticut side.

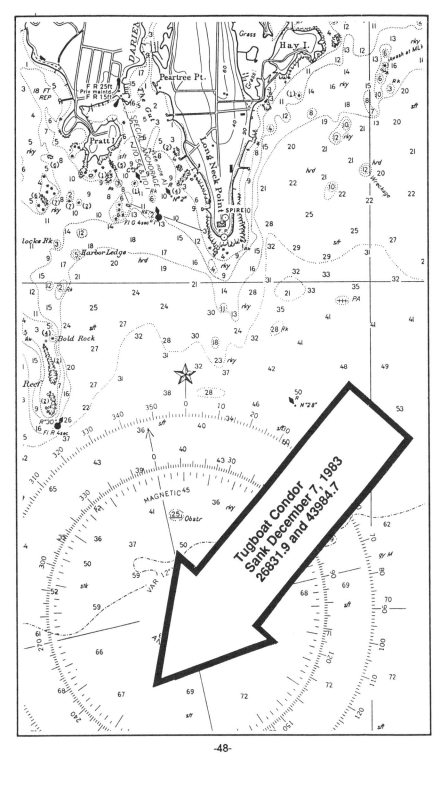

Tugboat Condor
Sank December 7, 1983
26831.9 and 43984.7

CHAPTER 22

Condor

On the evening of December 7, 1983, the 70 foot tug Condor left Portchester, N.Y. bound for Bridgeport, Ct. On board were a captain and one mate. According to a Coast Guard report on this incident the tug made a bare 3 knots on her voyage that started around 6 p.m.

If a two man crew on a 70 foot tug seems a bit thin, it should be noted the Coast Guard report stated the possibility of the vessel being involved in some sort of illegal activity. Around 9:30 p.m., a fire broke out in the engine room when the tug was south of Darien, Ct. The mate issued a mayday call over channel 16 on his VHF, giving their position and reported they were taking on water, presumably as a result of the fire. There was a stiff northeast wind at the time with 5 to 6 foot seas.

After the mayday call, the Coast Guard dispatched a cutter from their station on Eaton's Neck, Long Island and a short while later a helicopter from the Air Station in Brooklyn, N.Y. By the time the copter arrived on the scene there had been no further word from the people on the tug. Crewmen on the copter fired flares and spotted the men in the water. The cutter was given their position and around 10:30 p.m. had the two men safely aboard. They were taken to Nassau Medical Center on Long Island for treatment and observation.

The tug was by then on the bottom roughly south of Long Neck Point in Darien. Divers who visited the site the first year after the sinking reported very little growth on the steel vessel. Because of this there wasn't much marine life. But, after five years on the bottom, the Condor has started the natural chain reaction which turns something man-made into a fishing spot.

Fishermen can locate the tug at 26831.9 and 43984.7. We imagine blackfish and porgies can be caught around this wreck. As she deteriorates further the fishing will likely get better. People who know how to fish for fluke might try a drift or two around the edges of the wreck. Fluke, just like any predator in the sea, are attracted to sources of food. If there's bait around the tugboat more than likely there'll be fluke sometime from June through September. Fluke tend to hang around the side of the structure, laying flat in the soft bottom, almost invisible to the eye. Their eyes, however, are scanning the water above looking for a meal. Once the fluke zeroes in on his prey it can come out of its hidden position with a burst of speed if it chooses to do so.

The best bait for fluke is live mummies or killies as they are called by some. Live snapper blues make ideal fluke bait, particularly for the larger sizes, nicknamed doormats, since they look about the size of a front door welcome mat.

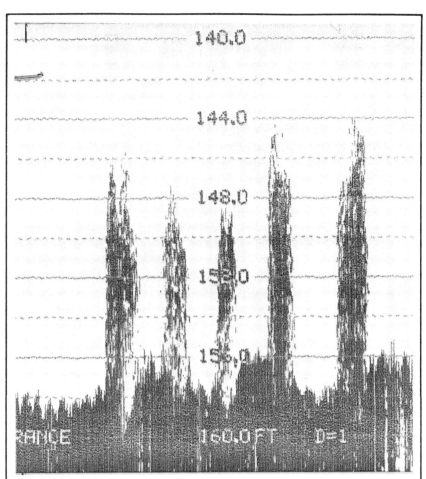

The hull of the freighter Coyote scuttled in the Boston Dumping Grounds on January 11, 1932. The decking has collapsed inward, leaving the hull with a U-shaped profile.

CHAPTER 23

Coyote

This wreck was the last one we researched prior to the printing of this book. Our hunt started when we received a number from a North Shore, Ma., fisherman who thought he'd found a wreck the year before while searching the bottom for cod outside the famed B buoy off Boston, Ma. What caught our attention was the fact that this same fisherman caught quite a respectable number of two to five pound cod off his suspected wreck. We took down the numbers and went looking for cod and verification in the summer of 1989. On a beautiful bluebird Saturday, Dave Jermain and I set out in his 23 foot Sea Ox to go wreck hunting. About two-tenths away from the numbers, Dave pulled back the throttle on his outboard and both eyes went to the chart recorder. Right on the numbers, exactly to the tenth at 13920.8 and 44266.2, a wreck showed up out of the soft bottom surrounding the site.

In the time it takes to write this, we had a jig and bait rig going below. The jig was grabbed on the second lift by a fish heavy enough to cut the line on the wreckage. Dave, meanwhile, was grinning over a chunky 8 pounder, just the right size for his dinner. In seven more drifts we accounted for at least two fish per pass. Once we cleared the wreck the hits evaporated. Once we motored back to the numbers the codfish started biting. That wreck was their home; they weren't about to go chasing about but if you dropped a jig or clam in their living room, they obliged.

On our trip home I wondered what we had just fished over. A check of the chart and the wreck list from National Ocean Service showed a symbol close by to be the freighter Coyote, sunk in 1932. With that information tucked in our briefcase, our next stop was the records section of the Mystic Seaport Library. The Coyote was built in 1918 at the Foundation Company. She was a wood ship, 267 feet long with a 40 foot beam, quite a large find indeed.

From 1921 through 1923 the Coyote had three different owners, the last being the United Transit Company. From that it would seem the freighter was not a money maker, or why else would she change hands so often? In 1924 the ship was abandoned at the dock in Boston. From that time until 1932 she rotted away. On January 11, 1932 she was taken out and scuttled at position 42-22-06 and 70-43-06 in the Boston Dumping Grounds, home to a lot of derelict ships over the years. Such ships, once located, will likely provide some lucky fishermen with great fishing.

Today the Coyote's decking has collapsed into the mud. What's left standing is the hull of the ship in a U-shape profile, a profile witnessed when a team of experienced divers visited and identified the ship in the summer of 1989. On the evening after the first dive we spoke at length over the phone about the wreck. The diver's last words before he hung up were, "she's full of codfish."

Cuttywow Rocks is an ideal spot to cast large surface swimmers for blues.

CHAPTER 24

Cutty Wow Rocks

What is the lure and attraction of a mass of rocks that roars, foams and belches when the ocean gets a stomach ache, that raises the hair on the back of my neck? Those same craggy knobs which rise up from the ocean's floor can bring a smile to my face when I cast an artificial lure into the turmoil and a game fish finds it amid the confusion of water, rocks and waves.

For the past two dozen years I have been navigating the waters of Buzzards Bay fishing my way from Sakonnet Point to Gooseberry Island, in Westport, Ma., often under the cover of darkness. Nearby Hens and Chickens Reef has always given mariners cause for concern, but since the Portland Cement Barge Angela went aground on the reef in May of 1972, her huge, faded red shadow warns us of the ominous presence of that reef, which has claimed untold victims over the past two centuries and beyond.

It is, however, innocuous places such as Cutty Wow Rocks, shown as an inconspicuous rocky location on chart 13218, which can put you under if you get too close to her dark, whiskered boulders just underneath the surface. Over the years I have come to trust my compass, but when I was making the return trip from Westport to Sakonnet approaching the midnight hour, I found myself unconsciously deviating 5 or more degrees to the south until I was well west of this hazard.

Such has never been the case when I was looking for some top water bass action or an opportunity to cast live eels along its northeast face in an attempt to pry a jumbo bass from its protection. It's a favored location for striped bass, bluefish and large sea trout which come here for food, cover and suitable habitat.

I can't recall a single trip here in over 20 years when we have not at least raised a fish. Cutty Wow Rock is located in Rhode Island Sound just off the Little Compton, R.I. coastline between Halfway Rock and Quicksand Point (better known as Brayton's Point, which marks the Massachusetts state boundary line) off Goose Wing Beach.

It's not located in any traffic pattern, as the preferred and heavy traveled route from Massachusetts to Rhode Island is the Buzzards Bay shipping channel which routes commercial and pleasure traffic from the Cape Cod Canal to Block Island and points west. Cutty Wow is primarily a local-knowledge location dotted with lobster pots and gill nets. Dive flags are a common sight due to the presence of groundfish and fair to good visibility.

The bottom rises from 50 feet up to 10 and 12 feet in some locations and the north face almost always breaks when there is a sea running. Casting swimming plugs amid the bearded boulders is very productive even during times of bright sun although early morning and evening as well as overcast days produce much better.

The southern edge of the reef is located at 14309.4 and 43974.3. Do not, repeat DO NOT go any further north beyond that point. Lay off to either side of the reef and cast a large surface swimming plug into the white water then hang on.

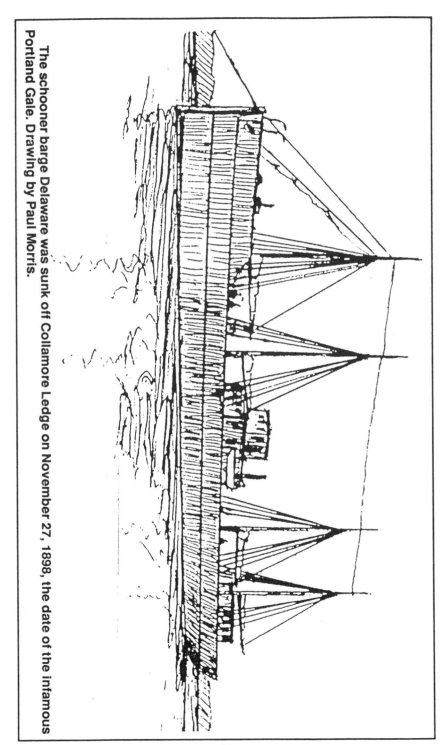

The schooner barge Delaware was sunk off Collamore Ledge on November 27, 1898, the date of the infamous Portland Gale. Drawing by Paul Morris.

CHAPTER 25

Delaware

One of the most famous storms to hit the New England Coast was the Portland Gale which struck November 27, 1898. This monster of a northeaster was responsible for sinking dozens of ships from Montauk to Maine. The gale got its name from the sinking of the steamer Portland somewhere between Boston and Cape Cod with a great loss of life.

Another victim of the blow was the schooner barge Delaware lost off Collamore Ledge off Scituate, Ma. The Delaware and the barge Daniel Tenney were being towed to Boston by the tug Mars. After rounding the tip of Cape Cod the tug and its tow labored up towards Minot's Light. Early on the morning of the 27th they found themselves trying to make headway against snow and wind aproaching hurricane proportions.

The captain of the tug ordered the barges to anchor to, hopefully, ride out the storm. At that time they were shipping alarming amounts of water. While captain and crew of the Mars lived to tell their story, both barges and their crews were lost.

It's assumed the Delaware's anchor would not hold in the face of the howling easterly. She grounded on Collamore Ledge and was smashed to pieces. The Tenney met the same fate, though not necessarily on the same ledge. Pieces of wreckage belonging to both barges washed ashore at Scituate on the afternoon of the 27th and the first incoming tide on the 28th.

Eventually the remains of the Delaware were declared a menace to navigation and blown up.

What's left of the wreck today sits at 13965.5 and 25714.4 in 55 to 65 feet of water. The wreckage is broken and scattered amongst the rock bottom but it does hold codfish. Divers told us they've seen small cod on this wreck well into July, so it's a good bet she holds fish in early spring.

Situated the way she is, under the lee of the South Shore of Massachusetts, it's possible to fish here in the lee of heavy southwest winds that could otherwise spoil a trip offshore. Fishing in the protection of the coast during a southwest blow is a favorite day saver for the charter fishermen out of Green Harbor, Ma. They can hug the coast to fish a lot of the rock bottom off Scituate. If there's nothing doing there they can work their way south, sometimes ending up as far down as Manomet Point, all the while being in comparative comfort and safety thanks to the lee shore.

The wreck of the Delaware might also harbor tautog, a species not widely fished north of the east end of the Cape Cod Canal. We suspect there is a tautog fishery in this area that's gone unnoticed.

School codfish like this are available at the east end of the Cape Cod Canal on the east tide, though not necessarily in the numbers of years past.

CHAPTER 26

The East End

Our codfish populations are not what they used to be thanks to years of neglect by people entrusted with safeguarding our fish stocks. The end result of such neglect was gross overharvesting, which meant less codfish for thousands of citizens of New England who fish for fun and their table from their own boats.

Ten years ago it was a good bet that two anglers in a small boat jigging the water just outside the entrance to the east end of the Cape Cod Canal could catch a mess of small cod on a day's outing. Today you can still catch some fish but numbers are down from the days we remember.

Ten years ago Charley Soares and I would launch his 23 foot center console bass boat at the Sandwich Basin in early spring before the tourist crunch bore down on the Cape. We'd run a scant quarter to half mile, shut off his engine and start jigging if we timed our arrival to coincide with the start of the flow of the water out of the east end of the canal.

If the tide was running hard we'd use regular bass tackle with 9 to 12 ounce jigs and tube teasers up ahead. That weight jig was usually enough to stay near bottom in a normal current. If we fished on stronger than normal tides we'd switch over to 14 ounce jigs. If we fished at times with slow tides or slack water we'd sometimes switch over to freshwater bass gear with very light jigs. Ever catch a 10 pound codfish in 30 feet of water on tackle meant for 3 pound green bass? The fight and fun might thrill you.

There wasn't any need for loran numbers as the fish were here and there chasing bait. Once we found a school we'd use shore ranges to stay atop them drift after drift. We would, however, usually start our drifts by drawing an imaginary line from the number three can over to the tip of the northern jetty on the Scusset Beach side. From that line eastward is where we'd usually find cod.

Our fishing started sometime after a break in the March winds right through the middle of May. As May waned, schools of three to seven pollock took over for cod numbers dwindling due to rising water temperature. If we returned to the ramp some Saturday in late May to find it full of cars, we knew our spring season was over.

If we arrived at the entrance to the east end to find the tide running into the canal, we'd run up to Manomet Point to jig the broken bottom south of the Manomet Point gong buoy. Often times we'd jig one to a dozen cod up there "waiting" for the water to start running out of the canal, by far the most productive time to fish the east end.

If you're an adventuresome angler, the east end will have cod off and on right through the winter.

The submarine G-1 was sunk off Taylor's Point on June 21, 1921, after being the target of an experimental bomb attack. Photo courtesy of the Peabody Museum of Salem, Ma.

CHAPTER 27

G-1

We wonder how many of the thousands of fishermen who run their boats down the East Passage of Narragansett Bay realize there is the wreck of a U.S. Navy sub not too far away? The G-1 rests in 105 feet of water just outside Taylor's Point on the east side of Jamestown Island.

The G-1 was commissioned in the New York Navy Yard on October 28, 1912. She was all of 161 feet long, a far cry from the giant nuclear submarines of today. Among her assignments over an eight year period were practice runs off Newport, R.I. and a then-record dive of 256 feet in eastern Long Island Sound. She participated in submarine exercises with a flotilla from New London, Ct., and also tested communications and sound detection devices off both Provincetown and Nahant, Ma. During World War I she engaged in two four-day patrols in the shipping lanes off Nantucket. G-1 was decommissioned on March 6, 1920.

Her last duty was as a target for some experimental bomb attacks. Eight such attacks were administered on June 21, 1921 by the Grebe in Narragansett Bay off Taylor's Point. The ship sank into 105 feet of water and was officially abandoned by the Navy on August 26, 1921. Today the wreck can be found at 14386.8 and 44010.7.

Master Diver Bill Campbell told us there's wreckage strewn all over the bottom but there's nothing left today that resembles anything like a sub. Such is the way with many wrecks according to divers. Either time or the wreck's dynamite or, in this case, a bomb attack reduced the lines of a lot of ships to piles of debris slowly disintegrating.

While diving on the G-1, Bill also investigated, thanks to a tip from a sonar expert at the University of Rhode Island, a nice rockpile closeby at 14388.4 and 44010.7. The sonar man found the rocks while testing a device in Narragansett Bay.

The G-1 wreckage showed up as a small blip on a color fish finder; the rocks nearby have a 6 foot profile. Both spots might harbor tautog in season as well as blues from time to time. The day we went over the sub for the first time there was a cloud of bait at midwater above her. Where there's bait, there's blues.

Fluke might also hang their hats around these two spots. We always used to catch bigger fluke in deeper areas at the junction of soft bottom and some type of structure, be it rocks or wreckage. The G-1 wreck might be a good bet in September when fluke are getting ready for their fall migration offshore. You might not get many fluke here but those that do take your bait might be the biggest of the year or your fishing career. Don't be afraid to try a larger bait; big fluke have mouths to match.

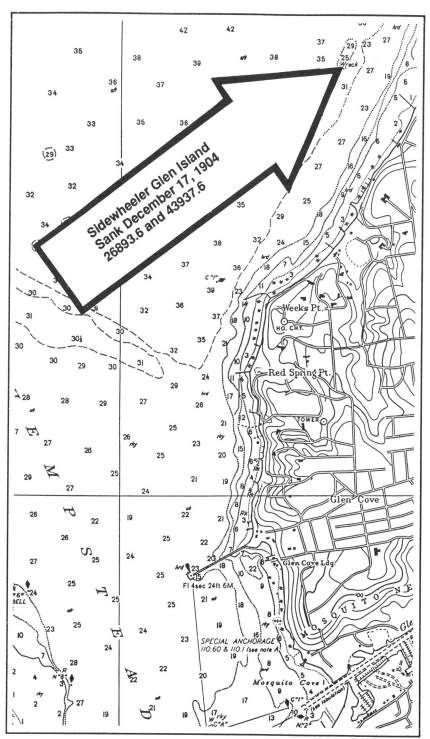

Sidewheeler Glen Island
Sank December 17, 1904
26893.6 and 43937.6

CHAPTER 28

Glen Island

It was a cold, clear December night in 1904 when the steamer Glen Island left New York, bound for New Haven, Ct. Off the Westchester County shoreline she caught fire which newspaper accounts stated started in the galley. The time was put at just after midnight on the morning of the 17th. Fire spread rapidly along the 238 foot wooden vessel. By the time the captain was summoned to look over the situation the flames had reached her freight deck. The Glen Island was a doomed ship. The captain ordered all passengers and crew into the lifeboats; being adrift in a cold wind was a better choice than burning to death. Of the thirty--some people on board, nine lost their lives in the disaster.

The survivors were in the lifeboats until picked up by a passing tugboat. The blazing Glen Island drifted to the North Shore of Long Island where she sank off the town of Glen Cove. There she remains today.

Different divers told us the debris from the ship is spread around over a wide section of bottom. There's a boiler, smoke stack and timbers, all of which hold fish life. The main part of the wreck lies at 26893.6 and 43937.6 in roughly 35 to 40 feet of water. Interestingly enough, diver Rich Taracka volunteered information he located some boilers close by the main wreckage of the Glen Island. Could they be part of the ship also? Time and some investigation by divers would be needed. The boilers can be located at 26985.6 and 43939.1.

We imagine the Glen Island and boilers hold blackfish during the spring and fall as well as everyone's favorite bait stealer, the cunner. You can usually get around the bait trimming antics of the cunner by baiting with half a green crab. Usually this brings hits from larger blackfish, not choggies as cunners are nicknamed in Rhode Island.

We also wouldn't be surprised if the wreck holds bass from time to time. Any structure in 40 feet of water fairly close to shore is a prime place for bass to hole up during the heat of the day. During the morning, evening or under cover of darkness they might prowl the shallows. But, during a hot summer day, you'll find them milling around some place they feel comfortable.

If you'd like to investigate the Glen Island for bass we'd recommend fishing a live bunker. Instead of just letting it swim around on top though, troll it deep with 200 to 300 feet of wire line to get in down near the wreck. Use a 10 foot leader of 50 pound mono between wire and 1/0 treble hook securely in the nose of the bait. If bluefish bite the bait in half, rig a second treble behind the dorsal fin. Connect the two hooks with a short piece of wire. The next pass over the wreck you can catch the short-striking blue.

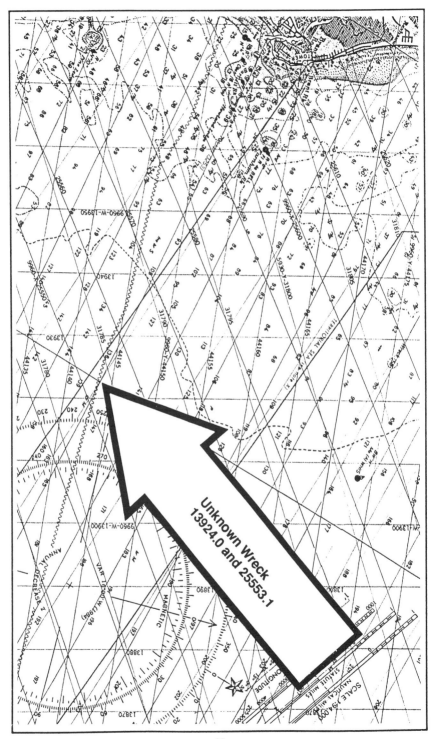

Unknown Wreck
13924.0 and 25553.1

CHAPTER 29

Green Harbor Numbers

Would you be interested in a computer print-out giving the identity and short background of most of the wreck symbols on current navigation charts? If the answer is yes, you can write to the National Ocean Service in Rockville, Md. to request the AOWIS Area One List. The loran numbers for the three Green Harbor numbers you're about to read came from that list.

Unfortunately, not all the wrecks have loran numbers provided so handily in the list. In fact you'll find a lot more accurate numbers right in these pages than the AOWIS List, which stands for Automated Obstruction and Wreck Information System. AOWIS will, however, give valuable background if you would like to start wreck hunting yourself. As we said in the beginning of this book, there are hundreds of wrecks off our shores going untouched by hook and line fishermen.

To obtain information for getting your own AOWIS list, please write to National Ocean Service, Hydrographic Survey Branch, N/CG241, 6001 Executive Blvd., Rockville, MD 20852. At the time of publication, the man in charge of the project was Mr. Mark Friese.

Among the wrecks listed in AOWIS, some do have loran rates included. Three such were found off the shore of Green Harbor, Ma. Oddly enough they are listed in AOWIS yet are not plotted on any charts we've seen. We checked out each of the numbers and found something on the bottom that looks like a wreck on a color fish finder.

The first one lies about 6.2 miles east of the number two nun outside the harbor. It looked like a smaller target at 13924.0 and 25553.1. Interesting is the fact that we ran over the numbers with the same 26 foot charter boat in October and then again the following May. The captain still had the same loran yet the numbers differed noticeably. We had to hunt around for 15 minutes before locating something previously "discovered." This shows to go you that even the same loran might not match up so you can imagine there will be differences from machine to machine, boat to boat.

With that in mind we can say the second Green Harbor number lies a short distance from the first at 13907.9 and 25537.7. The third number is roughly 7 miles east of the nun at 13911.9 and 25545.9. This third one is in the deepest water, roughly 160 feet while the inside ones rest on the bottom around 140 feet or so. What are these? Answers to that will await a diver descending. We do bet our printing bill for this book one or more of the Green Harbor numbers will hold bait and codfish in the spring. Next time you're out off Gurnet Point try one of these if weather conditions permit.

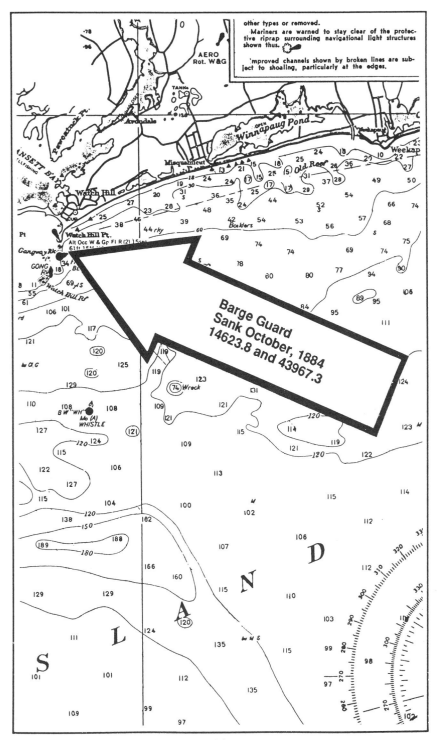

CHAPTER 30

Guard

Slightly outside the northern gong buoy which marks Watch Hill Passage off the coast of Watch Hill, R.I. lies the wreck of the barge Guard, sunk in October, 1884. This wreck was discovered and identified by master diver Charley Wolf of Sea Wolf Diving Systems in East Haddam, Ct.

The Guard was part of a string of three barges being pulled by the tug Minnie. Passing near the bell buoy, the Guard struck a rock, filled with water and went to the bottom. Newspaper accounts said the rock she hit was in 16 feet of water while the depth on either side was double that.

A wrecking crew was soon on hand to salvage the 1400 tons of coal on board after the barge crew had been taken to safety by members of the Watch Hill Life Saving Station. Such life stations were a common part of the New England landscape in the latter part of the 19th century. Manned by usually brave and hardy souls, they saved many a mariner's life from the jagged reefs and surging rips which are commonplace off our shores.

A week after the sinking, work on the barge was still going on. Some of the coal had been saved along with a portion of the rigging though the seas were breaking on the craft. In time she went to pieces.

Today the remains of the Guard are difficult to pick up on the average chart machine. Rising only three feet off the bottom, there's not much left to catch the eye, especially in an area with rocky bottom. Over the years fishermen have found the Guard but likely didn't know their lines were snagged on something man-made. Divers tell us they've found numerous fishing rigs fouled in the wreck. They also said they've found nice lobsters and usually see medium to large blackfish cruising about.

The remains of the Guard are at 14623.8 and 43967.3. Situated where it is, we'd recommend fishing it toward the end of the incoming tide when current isn't running at maximum. Blackfish will be your target in the spring though fishing for blacks seems to be better in the fall. In the spring, particularly if we get cold, rainy weather, divers report blackfish seemed to be thin and not really very active. Once the weather and water temperature warm up some there's more fish and they are more active. In the fall, divers say the whole area around Watch Hill Passage and Watch Hill Outer Reef is alive with blackfish of all sizes. Any wrecks in this fertile location will, of course, be worth fishing.

If you wish to give the Guard a try during the summer you might find some worthwhile scup (porgy) fishing. Several rocky areas nearby produce good quantities of these silvery creatures so the Guard might also. Instead of baiting with green crabs, though, try small pieces of FRESH squid.

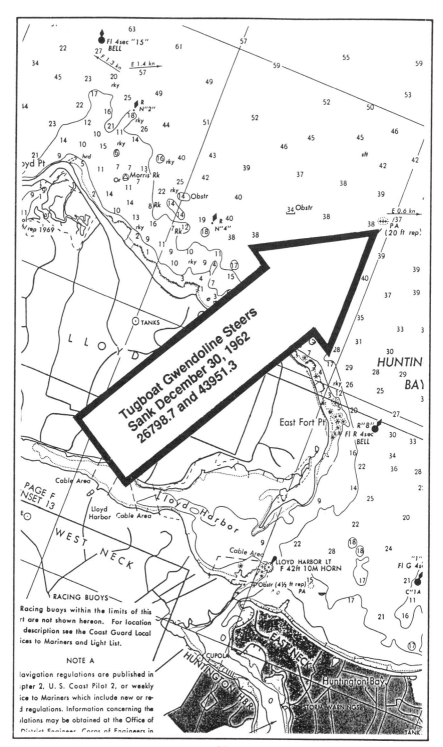

Tugboat Gwendoline Steers Sank December 30, 1962
26798.7 and 43951.3

Fl 4sec "15" BELL

F 1.3 kn   E 1.4 kn
57

R N"2"

Morris Rk

Obstr

Obstr

Obstr

R N"4"

E 0.6 kn
/37 PA
(20 ft rep)

TANKS

HUNTIN
BAY

East Fort Pt

R"8"
Fl R 4sec
BELL

Cable Area

PAGE F
NSET 13

Lloyd Harbor   Cable Area

LLOYD Harbor

WEST NECK

Cable Area

LLOYD HARBOR LT
F 42ft 10M HORN

Obstr (4½ ft rep)
PA

"I"
Fl G 4s

C"1A

RACING BUOYS

Racing buoys within the limits of this
rt are not shown hereon. For location
description see the Coast Guard Local
ices to Mariners and Light List.

NOTE A

lavigation regulations are published in
pter 2, U. S. Coast Pilot 2, or weekly
ice to Mariners which include new or re-
d regulations. Information concerning the
ilations may be obtained at the Office of
District Engineer, Corps of Engineers in

CUPOLA

HUNTINGTON HBR

EAST NECK

Huntington Bay

STORM WARNINGS

TANK

CHAPTER 31

Gwendoline Steers

On December 30, 1962, the 96 foot tugboat Gwendoline Steers was proceeding across Long Island Sound bound for Northport on the island's north shore. The weather on the day of the sinking was bad and getting worse but the captain of the tug had nothing in tow and reasoned he could make port before things really worsened.

Later investigation indicated the Gwendoline was seaworthy despite a grounding off Greenwich, Ct., a week before she sank. Not too soon before she went down her captain radioed the Coast Guard saying he was shipping water but the vessel was not in danger. A Coast Guard spokesman was later quoted in a story in Life magazine that wind gusts had risen to 67 mph with eight foot seas.

A short time after the first radio contact the Coast Guard radioed back but the skipper was still unconcerned about potential disaster. The station commander at Eaton's Neck Coast Guard had a visual watch put on the tug from a nearby hill. The final sighting in dwindling light and falling snow was 4:50 p.m. That was the last anyone saw of the Gwendoline Steers until 104 days later.

It took all that time to find the tug and for most of the bodies of the nine member crew to be accounted for. By the summer of 1963, seven bodies had been recovered. One of the first bodies found was that of a crewman encrusted in ice in a lifeboat. Divers and a Coast Guard investigation could only offer theories why the tug sank.

Today the Gwendoline Steers is at 26798.7 and 43951.3, not far from the entrance to Huntington Bay. The wreck will hold blackfish and some flounders in the soft bottom around the edges of the hull. Anyone who tries for flounders will have to put up with cunners attacking the juicy worms they send down unless they fish very early in the year before the cunners are up and about.

While the Steers isn't that far offshore, it can be far enough if the weather is threatening some day in late February or early March. It's not worth the risk to rush the season even if you've been cooped up all winter by the cold. Play it safe, especially if you're thinking about a trip across the Sound from the Connecticut side.

The tug wreck could be a bailout if the fishing grounds around Eaton's Neck are too crowded on a Saturday or if you wish to try for blackfish after chasing blues all day or vice versa. Our sources in the western end of Long Island Sound tell us Eaton's Neck can be a virtual log jam of boats on weekends. On the other hand, come a nice day in November, there's plenty of room to fish for bass that have replaced the blues of summer and blackfish on structures like the tug wreck.

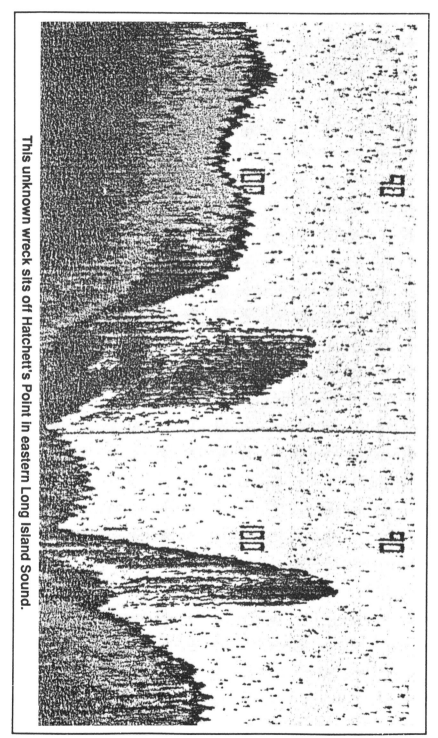

This unknown wreck sits off Hatchett's Point in eastern Long Island Sound.

CHAPTER 32

Hatchett's Point Wreck

One of the best sources for potential numbers for wrecks is captains of fishing draggers. These men are on the water day in and out; they must know where the hangups are or they will lose their net on what's left of an old barge, schooner or fishing boat. Getting to know one of these men is sometimes easier or harder than it may seem; sometimes you get an introduction from a source you wouldn't normally expect.

The salesman who sold us our house insurance inquired about all the books he saw on shipwrecks on one of his visits to the domicile he was about to insure. Upon learning of the project you are now reading, he volunteered that his grandfather was an ex-draggerman who knew everyone in a nearby port. A call to the man's grandfather produced an invite to go down the dock with him to meet some skippers still fishing. One younger man wasn't much help but an older captain, one on the verge of retirement himself, gladly offered some loran numbers in response to a polite inquiry. Several of the numbers in this book are the result of our brand of home insurance.

On another occasion some dragger numbers came our way through a diver who'd befriended a captain years ago. The diver would help with underwater work on the man's boat and freed his net from hangups on occasion. When the captain retired, he gave the diver his hang book, the result of 30 years on the water from the Carolinas up through the Gulf of Maine. It will take years of looking to go through what the captain gave his diver friend. One of the numbers, 26231.6 and 43982.1, was labeled in the log as a wreck and justifiably so.

This wreck lies off Hatchett's Point in the eastern end of Long Island Sound. She sits on the side of a rocky slope to rise about 12 feet off the bottom. Divers descended on it one fall day but the tide was just too strong to spend any amount of time surveying the area. Of the four divers who went down, three found only rocks while the fourth encountered a "wall" of sorts in front of him that he said was man-made. Lack of visibility in the pea green water and the force of the current made any further examination impossible. The identity of this wreck awaits further dives on a slack tide.

While divers couldn't see much, all did report seeing lots of lobsters and large blackfish. Here's another wreck to test our theory of summer warm weather fishing for tautog when other, shallower reaches of the Sound are devoid of blacks. They might sit out the summer in the 110 foot depths, waiting for the first cool fall northwesters before they'll be back in the 20 to 30 foot "shallows."

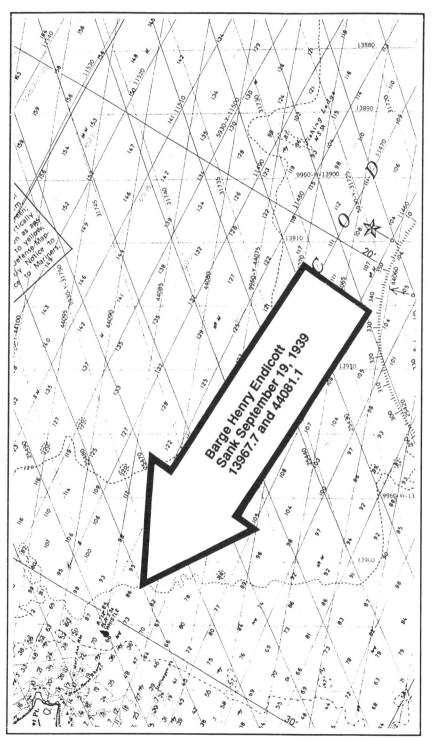

Barge Henry Endicott
Sank September 19, 1939
13967.7 and 44081.1

CHAPTER 33

Henry Endicott

Divers told us no one fishes the wreck of the barge Henry Endicott since they do not see any broken monofilament lines waving in the watery breeze. They do see small to medium codfish, red or mud hake, mackerel and tautog when the season is right. This is yet another case of a man-made reef gone begging for lack of awareness of the potential of shipwrecks as fishing locations.

On September 19, 1939, the tug Nottingham was towing three barges from Vinyl Haven, Maine, to New York via the Cape Cod Canal. Shortly after midnight the tug sent out distress signals to the Coast Guard saying it had lost one of the barges off Manomet Point on the South Shore of Massachusetts. Unfortunately the crew of the tug was unable to save the barge from sinking in heavy seas. While they attempted a rescue, they anchored the other barges then towed them to the canal at a later time. In this New England sea disaster no one was killed or injured.

The Endicott started her life as a schooner but, like a lot of sailing ships, she was converted to the barge fleet for her last days of service. At 191 feet long she is one of the bigger wrecks in Cape Cod Bay. The remains of this wooden ship are rotting away around the paving stones arranged like a loaf of bread on the bottom. You can locate the wreckage at 13967.7 and 44081.1.

Cod hang their hats here well into June and later. When the mackerel schools come and go in the spring and late fall they, too, stop off at the Endicott. Divers said they could look up at times and see mackerel swimming overhead. Once the water temperature warms into the high forties tautog show up on or near a boiler located slightly to the southeast of the main wreckage. Mud or red hake can be found near the bottom most any time of the year. They are good to eat though not nearly as prized as the cod or even the blackfish. Hake must be kept out of the sun for they have a tendency to go bad quicker than other fish. A sun-varnished, mushy, red hake lying in a hot fish box all day doesn't stir one's digestive juices. However, with care they do make a passable table fish or some might use them as chowder stock.

If mackerel are your target see what depth they are swimming at by watching for marks on your fish finder. Once you see a pattern at a certain depth, adjust your jigging with a Christmas tree rig to that part of the water column. You'll catch more mackerel than just random jigging, hoping for the best. If you drift out of the schools, crank up the motor to head back to where the fish were last seen. Don't just drift along hoping by chance to go over another batch. Some chum thrown out as you drift will not hurt your chances to fill your cooler with macks for supper or gamefish bait.

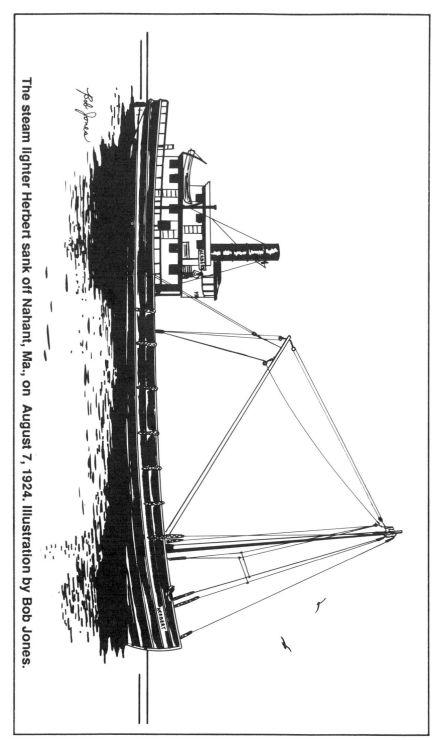

The steam lighter Herbert sank off Nahant, Ma., on August 7, 1924. Illustration by Bob Jones.

CHAPTER 34

Herbert

There's not much left of this steam lighter today: her wooden hull has collapsed after 60 plus years on the bottom of Massachusetts Bay. Her metal boiler, engine and forward winch though still provide enough profile to show up on the average fisherperson's fish finder if he or she seeks this wreck for codfish.

The Herbert started her "career" as a man-made reef on August 7, 1924. She was bound from Boston to Ipswich, Ma. as part of her duties for her owner, the Boston Sand and Gravel Company. Coming down the coast on her regular run from Gloucester was the steamer City of Gloucester. The weather at the time of the collision that sunk the Herbert was t-h-i-c-k fog.

About two miles east of East Point at Nahant, Ma., the City of Gloucester hit the 128 foot Herbert 20 feet back from the port bow. She sank in 15 minutes in 105 feet of water though, luckily, none of her crew nor captain was injured. They were picked up by the City of Gloucester and landed at Central Wharf in Beantown.

An investigation into the incident by the Steamboat Inspection Service found the masters of both vessels in violation of Article 16. As such, the licenses of both captains were suspended for 15 days. The damage estimate from the loss of the Herbert was put at $30,000, a considerable sum in 1924.

Situated where she is in Mass Bay, the Herbert is ideal for spring codfishing. Someone in a small boat could reach the wreck at 13961.2 and 44297.1 from any number of ports from Scituate on up through Manchester, weather permitting. We know fishermen who've caught small to medium cod off the Herbert in July so it's a cinch she'll hold fish in the spring. Sometime the wrecks in this part of New England will have small cod on them all summer, and, as a bonus, those anglers who wish to use bait can sometimes escape the dogfish by visiting a wreck. Sometimes, however, this is not possible. Sometimes, no matter where one drops a line there are green-eyed monsters waiting to take a clam rig or provide other aggravation. It's a common sight in the warm months to see dogfish follow a hooked cod right to the boat.

If you've located some hard bottom inshore you can usually get around the dogs by switching over to jigs. Unless you work the jig extremely slowly the dogfish will not grab it. Even then you'll still have -- from time to time -- the perplexing problem of unraveling a barker that's been foul hooked by a jig; the dog will come all wrapped up in line, leader, teaser and jig. It's a mess only a mother could love; the type snafu that causes hook and line fishermen to reach for a knife to hack away a good rig and try again.

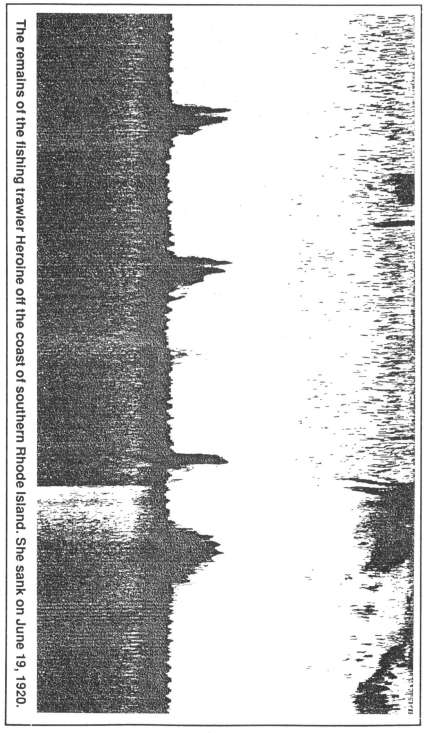

The remains of the fishing trawler Heroine off the coast of southern Rhode Island. She sank on June 19, 1920.

CHAPTER 35

Heroine

If you like scup (porgy) fishing this next wreck is for you. Divers tell us the Heroine is full of the tasty bottom fish during the summer months.

The Heroine was a 100-plus foot, steel fishing boat that steamed up from New York to do some fishing off the south shore of Rhode Island. Early on June 19, 1920 the ship sprung a leak. Captain and crew fought the rising water until it reached the firebox at which time the captain gave the order for the crew to get their valuables and abandon ship.

After a short time in the lifeboats the entire contingent from the Heroine was picked up by another fishing vessel, the Rose of Italy, which took them to Newport, R.I. where they were housed in the local YMCA until transportation back to New York was arranged on the afternoon of June 20.

Divers say the Heroine today rests on her starboard side with her bow facing east. There's wreckage scattered off to the south which holds fish as does the wreck itself. It will take a long time for this steel reef to deteriorate, making it a prime location for hook and line fishing for many years.

Old records state the Heroine sank approximately five miles west of Point Judith at position 41-18-18 and 71-33-42. The true position is 14525.7 and 43946.0. Unlike a lot of wrecks in this book, there is a symbol on current charts for the burial spot of the vessel.

A nice spike will show up on the average chart or color machine when you run over the numbers. In the fall you'll likely catch blackfish that have replaced the scup of summer. If we get some Indian Summer weather, the scup might hang around beyond their normal calling time. Don't overlook fluke fishing off to the edges or perhaps codfishing sometime after the weather cools in late October through Thanksgiving.

One species we haven't mentioned much is the winter flounder. They, too, hang around wrecks, usually in the soft bottom off to the side. Divers often report seeing flats in the sand around wreckage so if you're fishing the Heroine in the spring it might be a good idea to try a small flounder hook baited with soft bait. You run the risk of attracting a horde of cunners but you might also catch a whopping flounder. More than one diver speared an honest three pound flat for his dinner from a lot of our local wrecks. Divers further told us they've seen bonanza quantities of flounders hanging around some wreckage, fish that rarely see a hook. Their only threat is other predators, divers or a sharp draggerman who tows his net close enough to a wreck to catch fish but not in tight enough to snare his rigging. If a dragger captain loses a net he must either contact a diver or shell out considerable money for a replacement.

The author's son, Peter Soares, shows off scup and sea bass caught from the wreck of this 90 foot boat.

CHAPTER 36

Hilda Garston

Of all the hazards which lurk in the deep, the unknowns are the most dangerous because you can't prepare for them. In early March of 1961 the Boston Coast Guard issued a warning to mariners regarding a mystery object which may have been responsible for the sinking of the fishing vessel Hilda Garston on the morning of February 20, 1961.

Initial reports had the 90 foot steel scalloper, built at the Somerset Shipyard, coming to her demise by hitting an iceberg or submarine. This conjecture was later dispelled when sport divers discovered the ship was unscathed in her forward and mid-section but her keel and rudder were torn and twisted. This was reported as the result of hitting a reef, such as Old Cock Rock at Hens and Chickens Reef, which has been responsible for many a wreck in the cotton-like fog at the time of the sinking.

The ship was on her way home to New Bedford when she struck the mystery object and her crew of 12 and the captain manned her pumps for 45 minutes before taking to their dories. Conditions were so bad that a Coast Guard vessel dispatched from the Cuttyhunk Life Saving Station, not equipped with radar, became lost for four hours before finally finding her bearings. The crew eventually rowed to shore and forced their way into a summer cottage where they dried off and changed their wet clothing.

The boat's holds were filled with a cargo fo some 13,000 pounds of scallops valued at $6,000 in 1961. Both the hull and cargo were a total loss. The ship had been tainted with a hard luck image due to numerous circumstances which began with her launching.

On her maiden voyage she lost the results of 22 days' fishing on the banks when a fuel tank ruptured, spoiling her entire cargo. In 1958, an emergency auction was held to unload the cargo of 14,000 pounds of scallops so the boat could be hauled to repair a leak in her hull which cut short that particular trip. This streak of bad luck finally ended with her sinking off Westport, Ma.

The steel vessel sits today at 14238.8 and 43953.3 where she is home to many popular species of fish native to this productive area.

In our initial efforts to locate the wreck we were using ranges given by a diver and one of the salvage people who tried to raise her. The problem was the buoy given as part of the ranges had been moved several times. On our third visit to the site in the fall of 1988 we were drifting over the ranges when the chart recorder lit up with bait before the dark mass of the hull began to trace on the paper. Under calm conditions with very little tide we never got a good look at her as the three rods on board doubled over with tautog from 4 to 6 pounds. Two more drifts confirmed the hulk and the large concentration of 'tog around the wreck.

The last trip to the site, in August of '89 on the way back from a futile search for a tug down off Sakonnet Point, we stopped to bend a rod and get into a positive state of mind and took a few nice sea bass and some very nice scup. Punch the numbers for the Hilda Garston into your machine and they just might salvage a trip for you, too.

The steamer Horatio Hill sank in a collision in dreaded Pollack Rip Channel on March 10, 1909. Photo courtesy of the Peabody Museum of Salem, Ma.

CHAPTER 37

Horatio Hall

As with the steamer Aransas in an earlier chapter, the Horatio Hall was also claimed in a collision in the narrow reaches of deadly Pollock Rip Channel off the southern tip of Monomoy Island just below the elbow of Cape Cod.

On March 10, 1909 the Hall, after leaving Portland, Maine the day before, entered the channel on her regular route to New York. She carried some passengers and a cargo valued at $100,000. The steamer H. F. Dimock left New York, also on the day before, to enter the channel from the west to steam up the Cape bound for Boston. The two ships met at approximately 8 a.m. under foggy conditions.

The sharp bow of the Dimock crashed into the Hall on her port side just behind her stack. The force of the blow cut into the Hall about 15 or 20 feet, a wound that proved deadly. At first the captain of the Dimock ordered his ship to pull away but, seeing he could save lives by keeping his bow into the Hall, he ordered the engines run full ahead. With that, passengers on the Hall climbed over the bow to the Dimock's deck. The maneuver pushed the Hall out of the main channel over to the broken part of Pollock Rip. Shortly after the collision, the 297 foot Hall settled to the bottom with sea water flush with her upper decks. The Dimock, taking water through her bow, was run up on Nauset Beach to prevent her sinking. Four days after the accident, after some repair work, she was refloated to continue service.

Seven days after the accident the Maine Steamship Company, owner of the Hall, determined her a total loss and abandoned the vessel to the U.S. Government which ordered her blown up as a menace to navigation. The remains of the Hall rest, scattered about the bottom, at 13856.2 and 43897.0.

Divers told us most of the wreck is flattened down or buried in the sand but there's a couple large boilers that handily show up on a fish finder. The boilers and wreckage harbor jumbo blackfish as well as school cod; sometimes the cod are around into early July. Divers also told us they've seen bass over 40 pounds swimming about this area. A smart angler would then put out 250 feet of wire with a two ounce bucktail and pork rind to jig troll close to the boiler tops in roughly 25 to 35 feet of water. Large, savvy bass use rocks to block the force of the tide while they scan the waters overhead for a likely meal. When something comes by they rush out to grab it. We suspect they would use those boilers in a similar fashion.

If you like to fish after dark you might try some large swimming plugs also fished on the same 250 feet of wire, adjusted for tide flow. Blues will likely clobber those offerings also. It's a dirty job but somebody has to weed through the choppers in hopes of a jumbo striper.

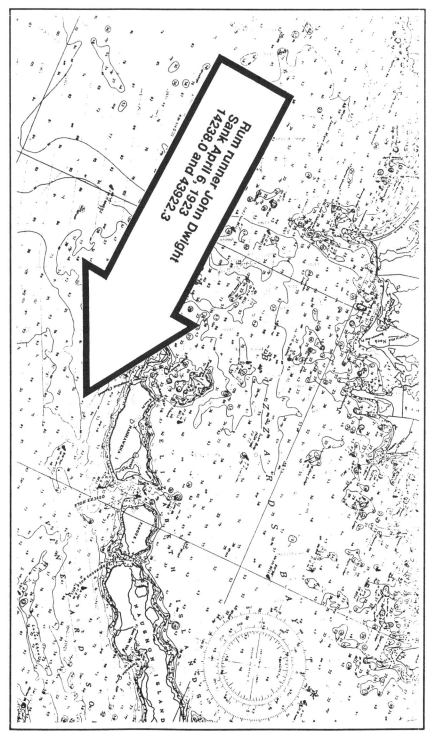

Rum runner
Sank April 6, 1923 John Dwight
14238.0 and 43922.3

CHAPTER 38

John Dwight

There are a number of mysteries surrounding the loss of the John Dwight, not the least of which is how to fish through all the cunners (choggies) which swarm over the remains of this 112 foot rum runner. We know where the wreck of the Dwight lies but a lot of the other details of the sinking and events leading up to it remain hidden in time and bloodshed.

The Dwight was built in 1896 in the state of New York. She performed various duties during her career including a stint in the U.S. Navy during World War I as a towboat and wrecker. Four years after the war she sat idle at a dock in Newport, R.I. With the onset of Prohibition, smugglers took her over as a rum runner sometime in late 1922 or early 1923.

On April 6, 1923 the lure of black market money brought the Dwight and most of her crew to a watery end. She was scuttled off Nashawena Island off the southern coast of Massachusetts. Despite a search the day of the sinking nothing was recovered except some barrels of cheap ale. However, the next morning the bodies of seven men were found floating in Vineyard Sound. On the opposite side of the Sound, authorities found the battered body of the son of the ship's co-captain drifting in a lifeboat near Menemsha Bight. It's generally assumed the men were the victims of some kind of double-cross that cost all of them the ultimate price.

Over the years there have been theories and a few articles on the mystery of the Dwight but to this date no one has answered the questions of who killed those men, who sank the ship and where did the person or persons escape?

The Dwight lies buried under 80 feet of swift water at 14238.0 and 43922.3. Divers told us she's pretty well broken up though you can still see plenty of brown or green bottles that held the ale lying about the bottom. Along with the bottles are large blues, fluke, tautog and p-l-e-n-t-y of choggies (cunners).

To "fish around" the choggies, you might try throwing a marker buoy on the wreck then start a drift with a bottom rig set up and baited for either fluke or tautog well before you reach the numbers. If you are using crabs, try a whole bait -- that, too, will help attract the larger fish to the exclusion of the cunners. There have been fluke to four pounds, tautog to eight and blues to 16 pounds caught here.

The blues were taken with a jig tipped with a piece of squid, an ideal rig for some nice sea bass which sometimes frequent the wreck in the summer months. When the blues are around, the cunners hide in the wreck lest they get eaten by the choppers. During those days you can bottom fish with relative immunity though the hungry blues are likely to eat anything including a small fish being brought to the surface or as it struggles near the bottom.

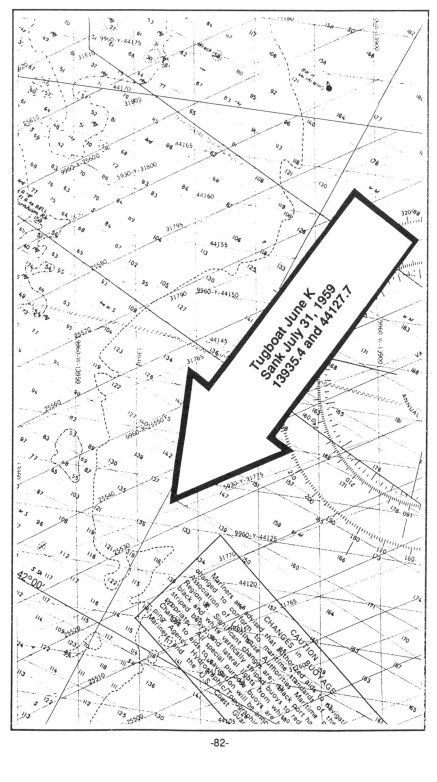

Tugboat June K
Sank July 31, 1959
13935.4 and 44127.7

CAUTION
CHANGES in BUOYAGE
Mariners are advised that the maritime standards of navigation are changed to conform to maritime standards of the International Association of Lighthouse Authorities Maritime Buoyage System. Region B. Significant changes are: black port hand buoys, striped black and white vertically striped buoys to red and black buoys and lateral lights from white to red. All special purpose buoys are appropriate to navigation will be amber. Changes to aids to navigation Hydrographic/Topographic. Ping Agency and the U.S. Coast Guard. the Mariner and

CHAPTER 39

June K

On September 30, 1958 the tugboat June K sank at the dock at Plymouth, Ma. There she sat until a contract was awarded for her removal by the Massachusetts Division of Waterways. On July 31, 1959 she was raised, pumped out, then towed to sea for scuttling.

The official position of the sinking was given as 82 degrees true, 6200 yards from Gurnet Light in 113 feet of water. The latitude and longitude of the wreck were listed as 42-00-39 and 70-32-03. In reality the tug was towed further out into Cape Cod Bay to 13935.4 and 44127.7 in roughly 135 feet of water. There is a symbol on current charts for the June K but her true position is quite a distance offshore.

Divers identified this wreck in 1988 after determining it had been dumped further out than specified. Why there's such a difference in location is a mystery. Someone probably related wrong figures which were then passed along from organization to organization.

The 68 foot tug is out on soft bottom but well within the range of a small fishing boat with moderate weather. It may be possible to locate some cod on this wreck in the summer after inshore locations around Gurnet and Manomet Points have dried up due to warm water. In the cooler depths cod might find this area to their liking throughout the summer.

One trick you might try on the hook of your bait rig is to place a small plastic skirt similar to that on the back of the freshwater bass plug, the Hula Popper. These skirts are sold for pennies in some of the bigger tackle stores. To put it on your leader just run it up the shank of a hook to rest on the top of the eye of a 5/0 Eagle Claw, a good choice for baitfishing. Next, put on fresh bait then lower away with sinker heavy enough to tend bottom. The skirt will flutter in the current even though the bait rig sits calmly on the bottom. A combination of the moving skirt and scent of the fresh bait often catches the eye of more cod than just a plain hook. On other trips there's no difference at all.

Most of the cod in this area will be under 20 pounds. Matter of fact, a 20 pounder is a good fish for this inshore spot so if whale cod are your quarry you'll have to push further out, more than likely to Stellwagen Bank or beyond for the 60 pounder of your daydreams. Such travel is sensibly restricted to seaworthy boats of at least 23 feet or better. Your 17 foot center console has no business heading to Middle Bank.

Other possible species on the tug wreck include red hake, mackerel, tautog or possibly some blues if the bait gathers at midwater. Don't be surprised if you find bluefish biting off small cod being reeled up. People like to eat baccala, so do bluefish.

The steamer Kershaw sank east of East Chop Light on May 31, 1928. Photo courtesy of Mystic Seaport Museum.

CHAPTER 40

Kershaw

In July, 1988 four divers found the bones of the 282 foot long Kershaw full of fish. They saw a lot of blackfish, scup, some school bass and a lone codfish. With credentials like that, this wreck at 14094.6 and 43922.1 certainly seems worth a fishing trip.

We were especially interested to hear about the cod. Charter captains from nearby Hyannis on Cape Cod told us they've had some fair years with school cod in Nantucket Sound though it wasn't something you could depend on. Dragger captains told us there's cod to be caught in the winter and spring in the reaches of nearby Muskegut Channel. With the location of the Kershaw right in the middle of those two bodies of water it might be an overlooked hotspot once the weather cools. It's in somewhat protected waters so an adventuresome fisherman might do some prospecting during the winter.

The Kershaw came to her location as a possible cod reef and very possible tautog hotspot on May 31, 1928 after she collided with the President Garfield. The Garfield was inbound to Boston after dropping most of her passengers in New York on the first leg of her trip from France. The Kershaw left Boston around 5 p.m. on the 30th for Norfolk, Virginia.

The two ships approached each other on a clear night around Hedge Fence Shoal. Amazingly, despite the fact that both ships answered each other's whistle signals, and each ship saw the other, they still met on a collision course. A writer covering the story for the Boston Globe labeled it one of the most amazing accidents along the Atlantic coast in many years.

Seven seamen on the Kershaw did not make it out of the ship. The rest of the crew and captain were rescued by lifeboats from the Garfield and other rescue craft on the scene. The President Garfield arrived at Pier 43 in Charlestown near Warren Bridge in Boston around 4 p.m. the next afternoon. The Kershaw was blown up with liberal amounts of dynamite since she was a menace to other shipping.

Today the twisted steel plates of the Kershaw sit in 65 feet of water east of East Chop Light on Martha's Vineyard. She'll hold tautog, scup, sea bass, school bass, flounders and other species as water temperatures rise and fall with the seasons. Most of the dragger fleet stays away from this large hang for obvious reasons, thus fish have a sanctuary until a fisherman drops his baited hook.

The Kershaw might be a good one to practice your anchoring skills. She's a large target; getting your rig atop something almost 300 feet long in 65 feet of water is easier than a tiny wreck in 40 fathoms. Your best position will be one that puts you on the edge of the hull.

The freight ship Kiowa was sunk outside Boston Harbor in a blinding snow storm on December 26, 1903.

CHAPTER 41

Kiowa

Northeast of Point Allerton, north of Ultonia Ledge and west of Thieves Ledge, unmarked on all current charts, lie the remains of the freight ship Kiowa, sunk in a raging snowstorm outside Boston Harbor on December 26, 1903.

The Kiowa's life was a short one, having been built the same year she was sunk. Almost at the end of her 14th voyage, her captain decided to anchor his ship outside Boston Light to await passage of the easterly so he could pick his way up the channel to Boston. The Kiowa was coming in from Charlestown, S.C. after a stop in New York. She passed Highland Light on Cape Cod on Christmas Day where she also encountered the storm that spelled her end.

Coming down the channel past Boston Light that afternoon was the SS Admiral Dewey bound for Port Antonio, Jamaica. Around 1 p.m. the bow of the Dewey cut into the Kiowa on her port side. The force of the impact had the Kiowa heeled over so far to starboard it was thought at first she would capsize. But the Kiowa righted herself to settle by the stern in spite of the fact that all watertight bulkheads were closed.

As soon as the bulkheads were sealed, the captain gave the order for distress signals to be blown on the ship's whistle. Responding to the call was Captain George Ham of the tug Cormorant. Captain Ham's vessel was coming into the harbor towing an empty scow on 600 feet of hawser. Using extraordinary seamanship, Captain Ham brought his tug alongside the Kiowa so all aboard could jump to safety. By the time the last man left the ship her stern rails were just about under. Shortly afterwards she sank to the bottom with only her stack and masts showing above a high tide. The Admiral Dewey stood by to render assistance then continued her voyage.

The Kiowa was a serious menace to traffic, so she was cleared to a depth of 30 feet by wreckers and their dynamite. Today fishermen can locate the wreckage at 13991.6 and 44265.5. A lot of the ruins of the ship are flattened on the bottom but there's enough to rise 10 feet in places. She's oriented north-northeast to south-southwest.

Codfish should be the main target here especially once the weather breaks in the spring. The schools of school cod that take up residence around the ledges of the outer harbor should find Kiowa "ledge" to their liking. The water depth is approximately 45 feet, perfect for some morning in April when winds allow a small boat to get safely outside the harbor.

As with other wreckage along the Massachusetts coast, we think there's the possibility of tautog. They've been caught sporadically from the jetties at the mouth of the Merrimack and consistently off Gurnet Point so we don't see why a structure in the middle of these spots wouldn't hold blackfish also.

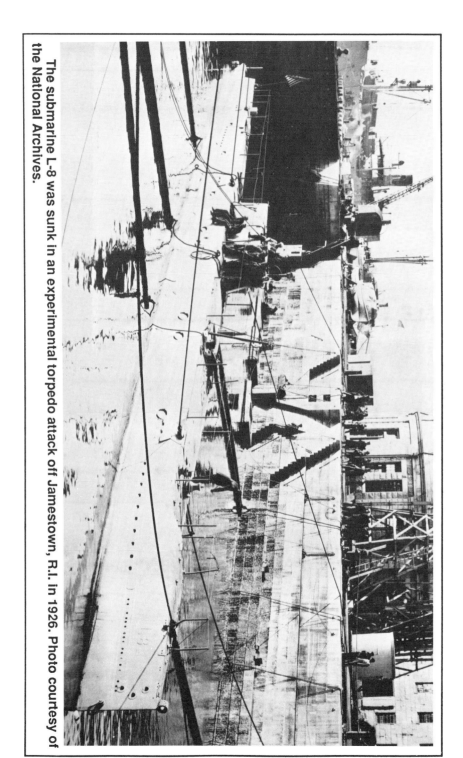

The submarine L-8 was sunk in an experimental torpedo attack off Jamestown, R.I. in 1926. Photo courtesy of the National Archives.

CHAPTER 42

L-8

If you were to run your finger due south on a navigational chart covering the area off Beavertail Point on the Rhode Island coast, you'd find a wreck symbol cleared to 85 feet a little offshore of the 43960 line. There lies the grave of the submarine L-8, sunk in 1926 in an experimental torpedo attack.

The L-8 was launched on April 23, 1917 at the Portsmouth Navy Yard in Portsmouth, N.H. She served in the Azores, Bermuda, the Caribbean, Central America, California and, finally, at Hampton Roads, Virginia where she was decommissioned in 1922. In 1926 the L-8 performed one last mission: she was sunk after taking a hit from a torpedo that would sense a metal ship making progress through the water. While one of the newer torpedoes did sink the L-8, a lot of them ran too deep or their exploding devices failed to function, fired prematurely or not at all. Unfortunately, the shortcomings were still there during the early days of World War II.

Today fishermen can locate the remains of the 165 foot sub at 14423.1 and 43959.1. She rests at a 30 degree angle to the bottom in 105 feet of water in a northeast to southwest orientation.

A resurgence of the cod stocks would bring cod here in the late fall through early spring. There are still a few hardy souls that keep their small boats ready on the trailer for that rare, mild, windless day in January when they try for some inshore action around Brenton Tower or perhaps the sub. Another stretch for fishing isn't too far from this wreck. You'll locate a nice rockpile from 14417.5 and 43965.9 to 14417.7 and 43965.0. The peak of this fishy bottom is at 14417.0 and 43965.8.

In the fall, either the sub or rockpile might harbor blues that respond to chunks of fresh pogies (bunker) fished on the bottom. Each fall charter boats from Point Judith and Snug Harbor catch a load of choppers on rocky bottom off Newport which isn't far away by either slow seagull or fast center console.

If blues are not your game, you might fish the sub or the rockpile for summer tautog. They might hold up in the cooler depths while shallower spots in Narragansett Bay go begging because of warm water. If the water is too hot for blackfish, perhaps there's some jumbo fluke lurking nearby. A live snapper blue (skipjack) sent down and drifted around the edges of each structure might bring the biggest flattie of the year. If you weren't rewarded in August, try again in September as fluke move down the bay. They stop off at spots like wrecks before continuing their trek to winter grounds offshore. You probably will not fill your cooler but the fluke that grabs an 8 inch snapper blue is indeed worth netting.

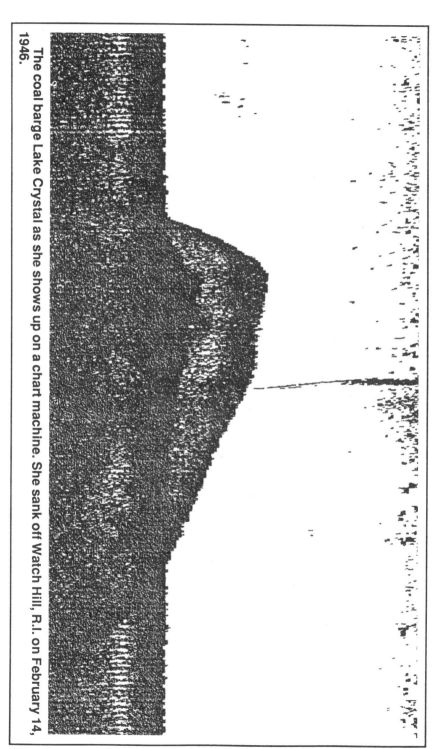

The coal barge Lake Crystal as she shows up on a chart machine. She sank off Watch Hill, R.I. on February 14, 1946.

CHAPTER 43

Lake Crystal

Early on the morning of February 14, 1946 yet another New England sea disaster took place off Watch Hill, R.I., scene of many shipwrecks over the last 100 years. About 5:40 a.m., personnel on the 253 foot coal barge Lake Crystal signaled the captain of the tug Nottingham that they were in a bad way; time was of the essence.

The captain of the tug immediately slipped the hawser to the barge then came about to take the eight crew members to safety. As the tug pulled alongside the barge, with heavy southeast wind blowing into a dropping tide, the large coal carrier flipped over to sink into 130 feet of water in Block Island Sound.

A high-powered searchlight was turned on the water to find survivors and the tug also sent out a request for aid from the Coast Guard. In time, the cutter Yeaton picked up a raft with three men on it. Two had perished in the winter weather while a third, the ship's cook on his first trip on a barge, was saved. He was transferred to a fast patrol boat for passage back to a hospital in New London, Ct. Of the eight men on the Lake Crystal, the cook was the only person to escape the sinking alive.

Six bodies were recovered; a seventh crew member was believed entombed in the barge resting upside down on the bottom at 14598.4 and 43944.9.

Today the Lake Crystal will show up on the average fish finder without any difficulty. She's now a reef approximately 260 feet long, 43 feet wide and 20 plus feet high. Scup might congregate here as well as tautog, fluke or possibly sea bass. In the late summer and fall when blues migrate through the Sound, this hump might hold the choppers at midwater. The big barge is an ideal spot for the small number of cod (compared to 15 years ago) that enter Block Island Sound during the late fall and winter months.

Not too far away from the Lake Crystal is the wreck of the steamer Larchmont which sank after a collision off Watch Hill Point in 1907. That wreck holds tautog in the summer as well as flounders seen by divers poking about for souvenirs and photographs. If someone wanted to fish that wreck after trying the Lake Crystal they could do so by heading for 14616.7 and 43949.4. Slack water or the slower stages of the tide might be a good time to fish either of the two spots.

Fishermen who look around might find other locations close by. We're told that the wreck of the steamer Metis, sunk in the 1870s, isn't too far away from the Larchmont as is the wreck of the tugboat Snapper, sunk off Watch Hill in the 1950s. If you decide to troll the area for blues, keep the chart machine running as you make your passes up and back. That hump you just ran over might be a promising fishing spot that will hold you well for years to come. Don't forget, get the numbers.

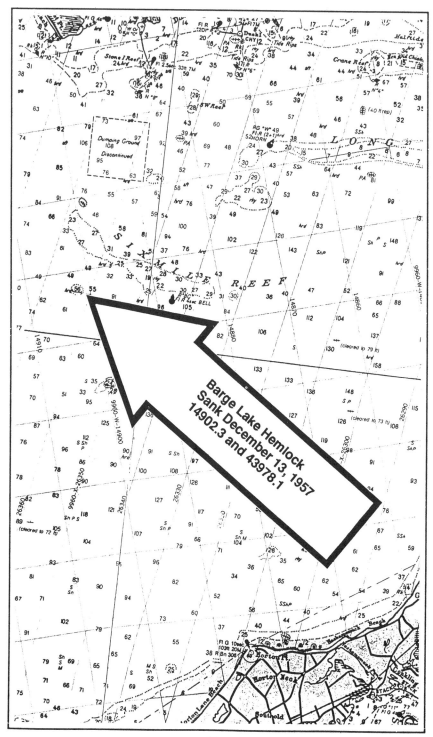

Barge Lake Hemlock
Sank December 13, 1957
14902.3 and 43978.1

CHAPTER 44

Lake Hemlock

Six Mile Reef is a popular fishing location in eastern Long Island Sound. Not far away from this productive reef sits the wreck of the 260 foot coal barge Lake Hemlock. Her last voyage ended on December 13, 1957 when she sank off the town of Clinton, Ct.

The Lake Hemlock was being towed by the tug Peggy Sheridan. Luckily, when the barge started to sink the three crew members got off without getting wet or hurt. She sank into approximately 85 to 95 feet of water between the western tip of Six Mile and the Twenty Eight Foot Shoal. A Coast Guard spokesman was quoted in a local paper as saying the barge didn't hit anything. She likely sprung a leak which caused her to sink. A couple days after the sinking, a patrol boat from New London, Ct. located the wreck with its sonar gear. Later a buoy was placed by a Coast Guard tender to mark the spot for passing tugs and barges, though there was plenty of clearance for other shipping.

Fishermen can find the barge at 14902.3 and 43978.1. She's a big target on a fish finder which attracts blues as the bait comes and goes. The Lake Hemlock is an ideal spot to drift over to drop a diamond jig to the bottom then speedily reel it about a third of the way to the surface. If there's no hit, take the reel out of gear, drop it back to the bottom and repeat the procedure until you drift away from the wreck. At that time, run back uptide to continue your drifts until the fishing peters out. On days with strong tides you might be better off waiting until the tide slacks off before you start jigging.

A six to eight ounce jig is ideal since you don't have to tend bottom but merely hit it or the top of the wreck, then start cranking. The faster you crank the better. A fishing friend of mine once remarked blues don't like something swimming faster than them so a hot rod jig is subject to chasing and killing.

The addition of a green, red, white or black tube on the end of the jig increases appeal. As you crank the jig upward the tube will spin, adding to the movement which convinces a hungry blue the lure is good to eat.

Most blues you'll catch with jigs will be under 15 pounds but, every once in a while, especially during the cooling days of fall when big choppers school to make their journey out of the Sound, you'll hit a bunch of gorillagators that will pull the mark to 15 pounds and beyond. Those fish do not come up so easy. They've been known to pull the eye right out of the bottom of some second-rate jigs.

On the tides when the blues are lining up to commit suicide, you should take only those you'll need for eating and toss the rest back. We've enjoyed relatively good bluefishing in New England for the last ten years. By tossing some back we just might keep our string going for years to come.

A German U-boat sank the barge Lansford and three other barges off Nauset, Ma. in July, 1918. Photo from the collection of William Quinn.

CHAPTER 45

Lansford

It was a hot, foggy morning on July 21, 1918 as the tug Perth Amboy steamed down the outer side of the Cape with a string of four barges in tow on a voyage from Gloucester, Ma. to New York. Just off Nauset Beach, hiding in the fog, was the U-156, about to make a World War I attack that would make headlines across the country.

Newspaper accounts of the attack quoted a deckhand on the tug as saying he saw something whiz by the stern. That something was followed quickly by two other similar streaks. At first the man didn't know what they were, but it soon became apparent the tug was under attack. In the next instant the ship was hit with a blast of shellfire that seriously injured the man at the helm.

It would seem the sub might have fired her torpedoes from the surface to follow it up so quickly with a shot from her deck gun. Other background sources for this incident doubt the sub fired any torpedoes at all on such poor targets; perhaps in the heat of the moment the deckhand was mistaken or perhaps some reporter got the facts wrong. In either case it was agreed by most witnesses that after shelling the tug the sub turned its deck gun on the four barges. One by one they were hit and sunk with the exception of the barge Lansford; it bobbed around with an air pocket in its stern until it sank the following day.

In response to the attack, planes were scrambled from the nearby Chatham Air Station but the bombs they dropped on the U-156 proved to be duds. Shortly after the attack, Navy brass were explaining to reporters from The New York Times the possible reasons for the bad ordnance. One author, Mr. Bill Quinn of Orleans, Ma., thinks the reason the bombs didn't explode was a softball game. Seems the enlisted man who had the key to the bomb fuse locker was away at a baseball game in Provincetown. It's the type answer anyone who has served time in the military can appreciate.

The sub escaped while the Perth Amboy was towed to Vineyard Haven. She was declared fit for repair and later returned to the sea lanes. The barges are still on the bottom, providing homes for cod and other ocean life. We don't as yet have numbers on the other three barges but the Lansford can be located at 13782.7 and 43981.6.

Large codfish can be caught off this wreck when water temperatures are right. At a little over three miles offshore of Nauset Beach, this reef is a very possible target for a small boat on a calm day. We know of several anglers who've had excellent codfishing on Crab Ledge, another inshore location close by, into July, so we don't see why the Lansford wreck wouldn't be worth a drop in early summer.

The side-wheeler Lexington sank off Stratford Shoals on January 13, 1840. More than 120 people lost their lives in that disaster. Photo courtesy of the Peabody Museum of Salem, Ma.

CHAPTER 46

Lexington

It was a cold night on Long Island Sound on January 13, 1840 when the side-wheeler Lexington began its normal trip from New York to Stonington, Ct., a passage of ten to twelve hours, a passage the ill-fated steamer would never complete. Before that horrible January night ended, 120-plus people had been burned to death or died in frigid waters.

Not too far west of Stratford Shoals the ship caught fire which spread rapidly through its wooden interior and the cargo of cotton. As the fire spread, the passengers panicked so it was decided to try to beach the ship on Long Island shores. Before that could be accomplished, fire burned through the ropes controlling the rudder. The captain gave the order to stop the engine but the fire drove the engineer away from his post. People on board faced the prospect of either burning or jumping into the icy waters. Some succeeded in launching lifeboats but a couple of those were churned up by the still-moving paddle wheel while at least one drifted away to be picked up empty the next day by a rescue sloop.

The people adrift in the Sound on all manner of "rafts", some of them bales of cotton, saw the blazing 205 foot steamer sink early in the morning. Only four people survived the tragedy. Three were rescued the next day while a fourth crewman miraculously floated on his cotton bale to Riverhead, some 50 miles away. His nearly frozen body washed up on shore two days after the sinking. It was reported he recovered from his brush with hypothermia and took up another line of work.

Officer Rich Taracka of the Greenwich Police Department is one of several divers who have investigated the wreck of the Lexington. In a letter, Rich stated the bow of the ship can be located at 26652.1 and 43962.8 at a depth of 138 feet. Another section of the ship, the paddle wheel, is located at 26679.1 and 43979.9 in 78 feet. Rich thinks there's two other pieces of ship on the floor of the Sound but he couldn't state for sure at this point.

The deeper section of the ship holds nice blackfish right through the heat of summer. At nearly 140 feet this section of wreckage might be tough to fish on a strong tide. We also understand some of the partyboats from the North Shore of Long Island fish there so that might also alter plans. A third possibility to keep you away from the deep part might be a dive boat anchored up where you wish to drop half of a green crab. If the latter is the case just go elsewhere and try the bow sometime when the tide isn't running too fast. Imagine catching a blackfish dinner off something wrecked on a cold night over 150 years ago. The fate of shipwrecks and fishermen is one likely to continue as more hook and line anglers fish for the secrets just off our shores.

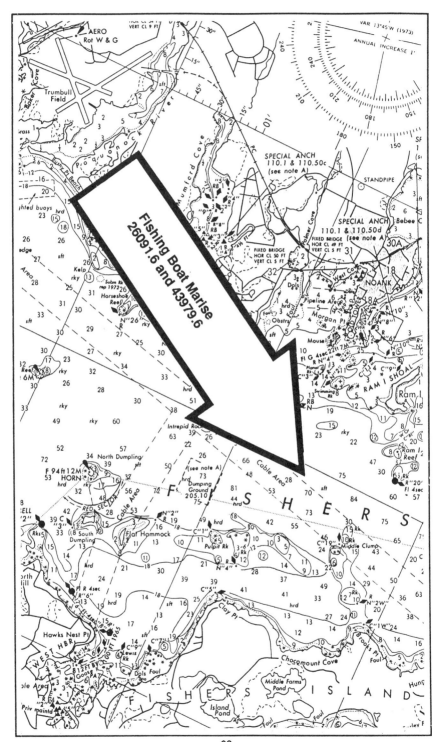

Fishing Boat Marise
26091.6 and 43979.6

CHAPTER 47

Marise

The Marise was a two-masted dragger that fished for years out of the port of Stonington, Ct., sometimes as far away as Nova Scotia. Today the remains of this fishing boat sit in 75 feet of water halfway between Ram Island and West Harbor in Fisher's Island Sound. The numbers are 26091.6 and 43979.6.

To research this wreck we talked with quite a few local people in the towns of Mystic and Stonington. One man at the Stonington Dock remembers a man in Mystic owned the boat for years but once he passed away, she sat at the dock with no one to take care of her. Mr. Luciano Bellastrini, who works part time at Shaffer's Boat Livery and has fished all his life, said as late as 1965 the Marise was tied up at Stonington. Later the ship went down in Fisher's Island Sound.

Some pieces of background we were able to get were that during the 1938 hurricane the Marise sank at the dock and was later refloated to resume fishing. Four years before the storm, the Marise was fishing 14 miles off Block Island where a pilot house from a fishing boat was brought up in the net. It was assumed the pilot house was washed off a boat by a large wave. The news of the find made its way all the way down to New York where it became a news item in the February 2, 1934 issue of The New York Times.

During our research it became crystal clear just how far our fisheries have slipped in 60-plus years. In the 1920s, some of the 50 draggers that fished from Stonington tried to relocate a large school of haddock one boat found five miles outside Breton Reef. Today you would have a tough time finding one haddock within 75 miles of the same spot. Other fishermen we spoke with reminisced about catching cod during the winter in the middle of Fisher's Island Sound on down to the deep water outside Bartlett's Reef. Such fishing today is mostly a memory, not because of polluted water but because of shrinking fish stocks.

Today the remains of the Marise rise about 8 feet off the bottom. Divers said only the bow still stands out on a chart machine; the rest of the ship is flattened. The wreck is an ideal location for porgy fishing in the summer months as well as tautog in the late spring and fall. If the tide is running too hard when you arrive, plan a return near the end of the flow right into slack water. You can then drift across the relatively small spot. Keep the drifts short as once you clear the wreckage you will probably clear the fish. If you are not sure of using your new loran to stay atop the Marise, toss out a marker buoy and use that as your guide. There may or may not be lobster traps around the wreck; lobstermen know full well the value of a shipwreck for increased catches.

The tugboat Mars sank off Manomet Point in a suspected collision on September 13, 1942. Photo courtesy of the Steven Lang Collection.

Mars

Often times during the Second World War, news of shipping disasters close to home was overshadowed by the tumultuous events abroad or it was hushed up for security reasons. News of sinkings came under the cloak of national security so as not to give aid and comfort to the enemy.

We can only assume such to be the case with the sinking of the tugboat Mars off Manomet Point on September 13, 1942. We've checked through the Boston Globe, Boston Herald, Plymouth Old Colony Memorial, New York Times and Quincy Patriot Ledger without finding even one inch of copy on the end of the tug. In spite of the lack of news, most wreck historians we spoke with said the tug was the victim of a collision with the tanker Bidwell, but to a person they couldn't produce any news clippings or magazine articles for background.

We further checked through shipping records at the Mystic Seaport to find the Bidwell docked in Boston the day after on a voyage from New York but that was all we found. A letter to the National Archives in Washington produced about the same results. A reply from a representative there stated their records showed the tug was the victim of a tanker crash but there was nothing beyond that. Somewhere, buried in some wartime archive, is the reason for the secrecy surrounding the Mars sinking.

Today the 117 foot Mars can be located about 2-1/2 miles east of Manomet Point on the South Shore of Massachusetts at 13956.8 and 44093.5. Divers told us her bow is gone and her wheelhouse is off to her starboard side. She sits in 120 feet of water lying northeast to southwest.

In October 1988 divers said they saw some nice cod down inside the wreck around her boiler. Smaller cod and cunners cruised the outskirts of the iron hull. To get the attention of the cod down inside, a diver and sometime fisherman recommended the following procedure. Anchor your boat so you sit just over the edge of the hull. Lower a bait rig down with fresh seaworms or sea clams to wait out the first hit. When you hook that first fish, reel it up a short way then let it struggle against the line. The struggle will attract the attention of the larger cod. Once they come out they'll find other baited hooks inviting them to your house for fish dinner.

The Mars easily shows up on a fish finder. It's not heavily fished, another case of a beautiful reef, sometimes full of codfish, without fishing pressure in this day and age of a shrinking ocean. Not all wrecks hold cod as well as the Mars but there are so many of these sites around that fishermen who take the time to seek them out will have the added benefit of fishing the choice wrecks as well as the old standby rockpiles.

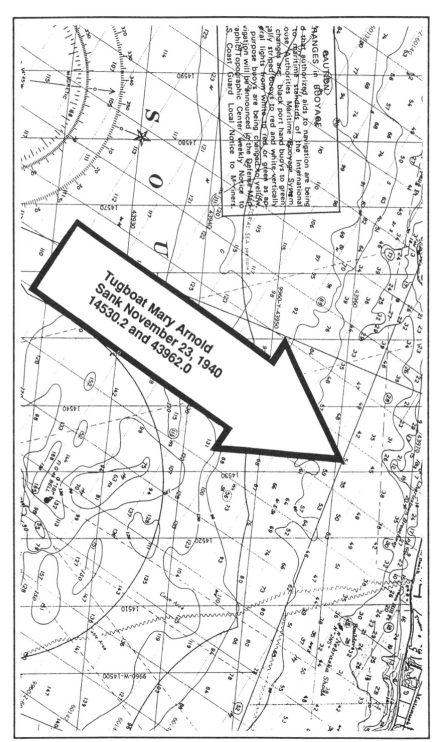

Tugboat Mary Arnold
Sank November 23, 1940
14530.2 and 43962.0

CHAPTER 49

Mary Arnold

On the evening of November 23, 1940 residents along the south coast of Rhode Island heard horns offshore and saw flashing lights. These residents later told reporters it sounded like a vessel in distress. The time was 9 p.m.

Two hours later the Coast Guardsman on duty in the Point Judith lookout tower noticed an S.O.S. being flashed from a ship somewhere south of Charlestown. Rescue craft were dispatched from Point Judith, Watch Hill plus the cutter Argo from Newport. When the rescue ships arrived they found the lone survivor of a convoy of three ships still afloat. Sunk two miles south of Charlestown Breachway were the tug Mary Arnold and the dredge Progress. Still floating, with most crew members from the sunken ships on board, was a lighter. Forty-nine years later the graves of the two vessels provides a home for tautog and other fish sought by New England anglers.

The next day debris washed up along the coast from Green Hill to Quonochontaug. Some of the wreckage suggested to the Coast Guard people investigating the incident that one or both craft might have been recently reconditioned. Perhaps one boat sprung a plank which sent it to the bottom, taking the other with it? The weather at the time of the sinking was wind and rain but a local newspaper article stated the storm "did not appear to be of a serious nature."

Whatever the reason for the disaster, anglers can locate the dredge in the area of 14530.0 and 43961.3 to 14530.1 and 43961.4. The tugboat, or what's left of it, lies in the area of 14530.2 and 43962.0 to 14530.4 and 43962.1. Divers told us there's machinery all over the bottom where the 110 foot Progress came to rest. The remains of the 70 foot tug are a pile of wreckage that took an experienced diver to decipher. Ten years ago the bow of the tug pointed upward but over time that, too, collapsed inward.

Besides blackfish, fishermen might expect scup to reside here, too. The nearby wreck of the Heroine is a hotspot in the summer for scup so we don't see why this one wouldn't produce also. During the fall one might try a chunk of fresh bunker in hopes of some prowling bluefish. If the topwater bait supply that particular October or November is lean, the choppers might turn their attention to all the small bottom fish found around a wreck. We've seen these blues linger past Thanksgiving, sometimes surprising a ground fisherman by eating a green crab meant for a white chiner. We've also seen people surprised by having a bass grab a chunk or diamond jig meant for blues on a wreck supposedly too deep or far offshore for stripers. Bass are creatures that go where there's food; most of the time that's rocks or the surfline; some days it's the bones of a shipping mishap.

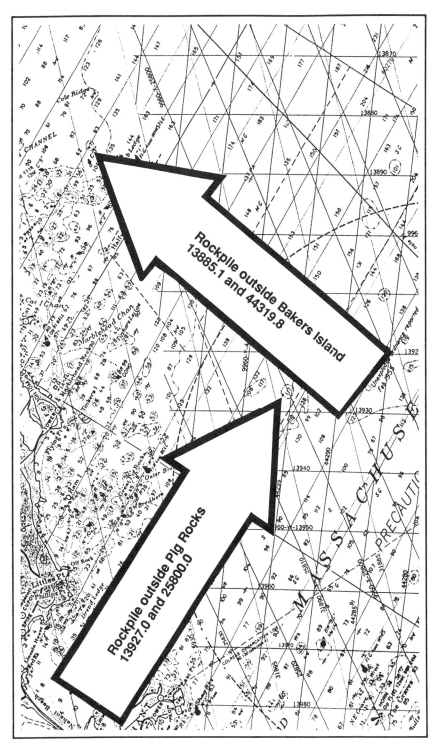

Rockpile outside Bakers Island
13885.1 and 44319.8

Rockpile outside Pig Rocks
13927.0 and 25800.0

CHAPTER 50

Massachusetts Bay Rockpiles

Massachusetts Bay is dotted with rockpiles that harbor fish. The following is but a small selection of what's available in that body of water. A fisherman who likes to explore can find dozens of others merely by eyeballing the high spots off a chart then running a grid pattern back and forth until he locates a hump. Almost any hill will, at one time or another, hold codfish either for the jigger or the person who chooses to fish with a bait rig.

13885.1 and 44319.8
47 Hill outside Baker's Island

13883.3 and 44287.1
101 Hill outside Marblehead

13894.6 and 44288.3
115 Hill outside Marblehead

13927.0 and 25800.0
117 Hill outside Pig Rocks

13927.0 and 25754.0
119 Hill outside B Buoy

13892.2 and 44268.9
Small Rockpile outside B Buoy

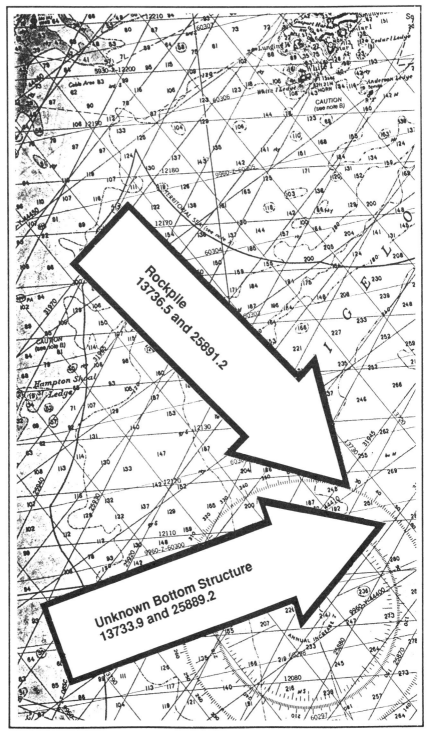

Rockpile
13736.5 and 25891.2

Unknown Bottom Structure
13733.9 and 25889.2

CHAPTER 51

Newburyport Numbers

This section of numbers is within the reach of a fisherman in a moderate size boat on a good day. Before shoving off, we'd like to emphasize safety once more, especially early in the year when cabin fever might tempt you to push the weather beyond the capacity of your boat. Some of these numbers are a long walk home if it blows up the wrong way.

13736.5 and 25891.2
Large rockpile

13733.9 and 25889.2
Either wreck or rockpile

13779.6 and 44411.2
Obstruction on bottom

13715.5 and 44422.7
Possible wreck F/V Lucretia (unverified)

13650.7 and 44335.4
Unverified wreck

13657.2 and 44353.2
Possible groundfishing near The Cove

The steamer Onondaga sank off Watch Hill, R.I. on June 28, 1918. Here she's shown aground on Cape Cod in 1907, one of two earlier mishaps. Photo courtesy of the Peabody Museum of Salem, Ma.

CHAPTER 52

Onondaga

During the summer and fall months, divers told us, they've seen large bass cruising about the jagged remains of the 275 foot steamer Onondaga. She sits in 35 to 45 feet of water inside the Outer Reef off Watch Hill Light, an area that's claimed many ships in the last 100 years.

On June 28, 1918 the steamer was enroute from Boston to Charleston, S.C. After coming down the outer portion of Cape Cod she was ordered to take the inside route through Vineyard and Long Island Sounds because of the threat from World War I U-boats. The inside passage was the ship's undoing as the captain was not familiar with the terrain. He mistook Watch Hill Light for the lighthouse at Race Rock, so he proceeded over what he thought was deep water. The Onondaga struck the reef at Watch Hill at cruising speed. The impact opened up her seams and sent her over the rocks to sink in the deeper water on the shoreward side. Thankfully, all aboard were rescued by personnel from the Watch Hill Lifesaving Station. In time the steamer was blown up after some of her cargo was removed.

Prior to her sinking at Watch Hill, the Onondaga had two earlier brushes with disaster. In January of 1907, the ship ran up on the beach at Cape Cod. Her cargo was taken off and she was refloated to resume service. In August, 1915, she rammed into the old schooner Franconia off Chatham, Ma. The Franconia, though damaged, made her way to Boston where she was declared a total loss. Once more, though, the 'Daga continued on. Her third and last strike came off the Rhode Island coast. Today fishermen can pay their respects to the remains at 14627.7 and 43966.4.

During the last hour of a night ebb tide about four days before to four days after the full moon a bass fisherman might drop a weighted live eel down to drift it across the top of the wreck. You might have to fish your way through some blues but the bass are there. Once you hook that 40 pounder you then have to keep it away from the jagged hull. Then there's the matter of the Outer Reef. The rocks break the surface and, on an ebb tide, you'll be drifting in that direction, a drift you do not want to complete. However, with very little current you can fight a fish yet still have enough time to keep away from the infamous rocks.

If drifting isn't your game, you could anchor up to fish chunks of fresh pogies around the wreck. Blues might grab your bait as well as bass of various sizes. If you choose October and November to anchor on this wreck it would be in your best interest to fish green crabs here. The 'Daga is wall-to-wall tautog when the frost is on the pumpkin. If they do not bite well during the strength of the tide, make it a point to return the last couple hours...

Horseshoe Shoal, not far from the dynamited remains of PC 1203, offers good surface fishing for blues.

CHAPTER 53

PC 1203

In 1949 the Navy deliberately grounded a 173 foot, steel Patrol Craft, the PC1203, on Horseshoe Shoals in Nantucket Sound as a bombing target. From then until 1961, the area was designated as a Danger Zone to be avoided, especially by the weekend boater. After 1961 the Danger Zone was withdrawn because, we assume, the Navy no longer needed the 1203 as a target. On July 18, 1963 a buoy was established to mark the wreck for safety reasons.

From 1963 until 1971 a fisherman in a sportfishing boat may have bumped or scraped the hulk while bluefishing on productive Horseshoe Shoals but no harm came to anyone until a 34 foot pleasure boat hit the submerged wreck. On October 1, 1971, eight people were aboard the Ad Lib II when it ran into the bones of the PC1203. In the end, six were rescued but, unfortunately, two lost their lives.

The cry over the incident caused Navy and Coast Guard officials to decide the wreck must be blown up. In November, 1971, 300 pounds of dynamite were used to destroy the super structure and a large part of the hull. Twenty-eight years later all the local fishermen we quizzed thought the hull completely flattened against the bottom or that it was one of those wrecks that sands in, then uncovers during a winter storm. To a man they agreed with Captain Dennis Sabo of the charterboat Peptide that the wreck wasn't worth much as a fishing spot. However, all was not lost with our research on this ship disaster.

Very close to the PC1203 one will find a high spot on Horseshoe Shoals that can offer absolutely dynamite topwater fishing for blues. If someone would head for 14029.2 and 43921.8, he or she would see the location east of those numbers. The preferred method is to drift just north or south of the high ground, tossing poppers into the breaking water. Blues hug the shoal at times while others may be out in the slightly deeper water your boat is in. On other days you'll have to break out the wire line to check deeper areas.

When blues are thick you can take off the treble hooks of your Gibbs Pencil Poppers or your Smoker Baits or Atom poppers and replace them with one large single hook on the back eye. You'll still enjoy the explosive strikes of surface-feeding blues, but when you go to unhook them, it will be a lot easier on you, your boat and your guests with just a single hook to undo. A single hook is also safer since you don't have the thrashing, bouncing bluefish jumping about your cockpit with a face full of trebles. If you take a priest to the fish it will not be eligible for release. The best solution for safety, excitement and conservation is the single hook popper.

Stern section of the tanker Pendleton off Monomoy Island in 1952. Photo courtesy of the William Quinn collection.

CHAPTER 54

Pendleton

One of the greatest Coast Guard rescues in modern times took place on February 19, 1952 when four enlisted men in a 36 foot motorized lifeboat took 32 crew members off the stern section of a broken tanker, the Pendleton, in a raging storm off Chatham, Ma.

The story started earlier that day when the Pendleton split under pressure from heavy seas and northeast winds. The location given at the time of the split was 10 to 15 miles off Highland Light on Cape Cod. At the time the Pendelton broke apart, another tanker, the Fort Mercer, also split, so the Coast Guard had to deal with the four halves of not one but two ships in a bad way. The Fort Mercer is a story in herself but we'll confine our efforts here to the Pendleton.

Eight members of the Pendleton crew, including the captain, were on the bow section. The next morning that half washed up on the broken part of Pollock Rip. A later search of the bow revealed only one body so it was assumed the others lost their lives in trying to launch a life raft. The stern section drifted past Chatham late in the afternoon of the 19th. By the time help was actually on the way to the ship she'd drifted further south into the waiting darkness.

Imagine the courage of the four Coast Guardsmen to first get their 36 footer across the God forsaken Chatham Bar at the old Chatham inlet on a winter night with 40 to 50 mph northeast winds blowing up into a falling tide. If that weren't enough, the crossing of the bar knocked out the compass and radio, so, using only the prevailing wind as a guide, Boatswain's Mate Bernard Webber succeeded in locating the ship then, one by one, getting all the men off but one, the 300 pound ship's cook who was crushed between the lifeboat and the tanker after he mis-timed his jump from a ladder hung over the side. His bulk was so much that men in the lifeboat couldn't hang on to him after he plunged into the surging water. Later that night Boatswain Webber brought the lifeboat back into Chatham with 36 men aboard. It was truly a rescue that will live in Coast Guard honor rolls for years to come.

The stern of the Pendleton grounded the next morning just off Monomoy Island below Chatham. Her hulk rested above the water until the Blizzard of 1978 knocked it over. Afterwards a lot of her wreckage was removed, though there are still pieces of the hull on the bottom at 13867.7 and 44914.0.

The Pendleton wreck is a bass wreck. Divers continually report large bass which should respond to a live pogy dropped over their haunt or trolled past. If the tide is running they'll likely be on the downtide side of the wreck using it to block the current. If the tide is slack you might find the bass anywhere.

The coastal tanker Pinthis sank in a devastating collision off Scituate, Ma. on June 10, 1930.

CHAPTER 55

Pinthis

Fog was responsible for this sinking, causing a collision between a steamer and a smaller coastal tanker off Fourth Cliff on the South Shore of Massachusetts. The date was June 10, 1930.

The steamer Fairfax left Boston bound for Norfolk, Va. Coming up the coast, after clearing the Cape Cod Canal, was the 206 foot tanker Pinthis enroute to Bangor, Me. from Fall River. She had 12,000 barrels of oil in her hold. In the dense fog the larger Fairfax struck the tanker on her port side, causing a devastating explosion. Less than 20 minutes after the crash, the flaming tanker capsized, taking all members of her 19 man crew with her. The sea was ablaze at the time. Even though the tanker went to the bottom in 100 feet of water the oil coming out of her caused the water "to burn" several days after she sank.

The burning oil was washed onto the bow of the Fairfax and from there spread to her superstructure. Some members of her crew and passengers were engulfed in the flames, others panicked and leaped into the flaming ocean. The bodies were picked up the next day by a fishing trawler which returned them to Boston. In time, thanks to the courageous efforts of some passengers and crew which kept their heads, the fire was put out. Eighteen hours after she left Boston the Fairfax returned, her upper decks charred, her bow with a gaping hole below the water line. In all, 47 people either drowned or burned to death as a result of the accident.

Today the Pinthis sits upside down on the bottom at 13924.4 and 44175.3. She holds a lot of codfish from time to time, notably in the spring and possibly in the fall or during the winter months. Years ago, charter captains like Roger Jarvis would take parties to this wreck to catch codfish and usually a nice mess of haddock. Today you'd fish a long time before encountering many haddock on the Pinthis but codfishing can be quite good. Please keep in mind this is also a popular dive spot so if there's a boat with a dive flag anchored up ahead of you try another spot.

All around the Pinthis is good rocky bottom which holds cod and sometimes a couple wolffish. All the rocky bottom off Scituate is a prime target for the man with a small boat. A lot of the many humps and dips can be eyeballed off a chart with loran overlay with reasonable accuracy. Places like Stellwagen Ledges (not to be confused with Stellwagen Bank) and the bottom to the east are all worth a look. If you mark some fish, drop a jig down and await results. Like other locations along this shore, most of the cod you'll catch will be under 20 pounds but there's always a chance, especially as you head out into somewhat deeper water, that a 50 pounder might be looking over your jig.

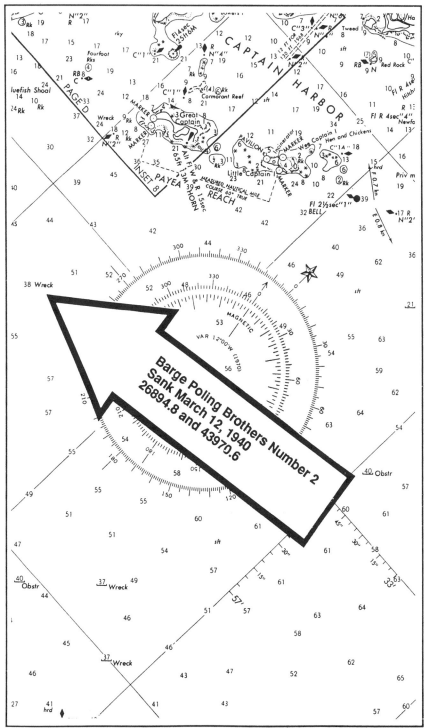

CHAPTER 56

Poling Brothers Number Two

Not far outside of the fishing grounds around Great Captain Island in the western part of Long Island Sound sits the wreck of the oil barge Poling Brothers Number Two, sunk on February 7, 1940.

Lying in 70 feet of water, this "reef" is 116 feet long with an 18 foot beam. In researching this one we came up against a stone wall. Only two local papers carried any news of the sinking and one of those had thrown out all its back records. Another paper, on microfilm in the Greenwich Public Library, was our hope until we found out some low-life made off with the exact roll of microfilm needed. Such thievery is nothing new in the times in which we live.

Anyway, we relied on Officer Rich Taracka of the Greenwich Police Marine Squad for what information we could dig up. The barge sits upright on the bottom. If you've got your chart machine tuned right you should see the pilot house atop the wreck on the stern. During one of his many dives to the wreck, Rich noticed charred wood so perhaps a fire was the cause of the sinking. But, until the library replaces the missing roll of microfilm, we'll just have to wonder.

As we've noted elsewhere in this book, barge founderings were common occurrences in New England waters, especially in such a heavily traveled area as the western end of the Sound. Because of that, the news of the sinkings rated limited space in the local papers and nothing in a large daily like the Times. The sinking received such little press that even official versions of the date are in question. Records at the National Ocean Service put the date at February 7, 1940, while the Vessels Lost Section of the 1940 edition of Merchant Vessels of the United States lists March 12 as the correct one.

In any event the wreck can be found at the intersection of 26894.8 and 43970.6. Fishermen can expect tautog, perhaps some jumbos if another fishing or dive boat isn't there before you. In the soft bottom adjacent to the Number Two will be flounders, sometimes big ones. A two pound flounder is a large one for western Long Island Sound; here's a place you might just catch one that size.

The British freighter Port Hunter sank on Hedge Fence Shoal on November 2, 1918.

CHAPTER 57

Port Hunter

On the morning of November 2, 1918 the 320 foot British freighter Port Hunter was proceeding through Nantucket Sound enroute from Boston to New York to join up with a convoy headed to France with war supplies. Remember, World War I was raging at the time.

Before this large ship reached her destination she was struck on the port side by the tug Covington. Efforts to save the ship failed, eventually she sank to the bottom of the Sound on Hedge Fence Shoal off West Chop on Martha's Vineyard.

At first the steamer's decks were not that far below the surface. Dollar conscious Yankees became aware of the salvage potential and went to work with grapnel hooks and quahog rakes. Thanks to those efforts the commerce of local communities received an influx of trading in olive drab shirts, rubber boots and woolen underwear that brought anywhere from ten cents to three dollars per item.

The government stepped in to halt the unauthorized pilferage of war goods. Some of the unauthorized goods "mysteriously" found their way into local stores, some of which chose to ignore an order for their return; some shops in New Bedford were raided as a result of failure to comply.

The first authorized salvage began in 1919 which brought up a lot of clothing that then had to be laundered then was auctioned off at Commonwealth Pier, now World Trade Center, in Boston. In the end, the government only recovered about 20% of the value of the material. In 1961, another salvage effort got underway, this one to bring up scrap metal, a venture that provided a $100,000 profit for the Boston attorney who funded the venture.

Since the first people raked up material from the deck of the Port Hunter, the ship has settled deeper and deeper. Today her bow is about 25 feet down while the stern is in approximately 70 feet of water. The loran numbers are 14097.7 and 43930.7.

Bass and blues take up feeding stations around the wreck in a tide which hums across this area. I wonder if many of the trollers that fish Hedge Fence Shoal realize that one of the large tide boils there is created by something man-made that is 320 feet long that's been sitting there for more than 60 years.

Trollers might try a bucktail and pork rind on 200 feet of wire line to reach the gamefish on the bow. Once the tide eases off fishermen interested in ground fish like sea bass might drop a baited hook around the stern. The section along the port side of the forward part of the ship, where the tug crashed into the hull, is home to more sea bass and scup.

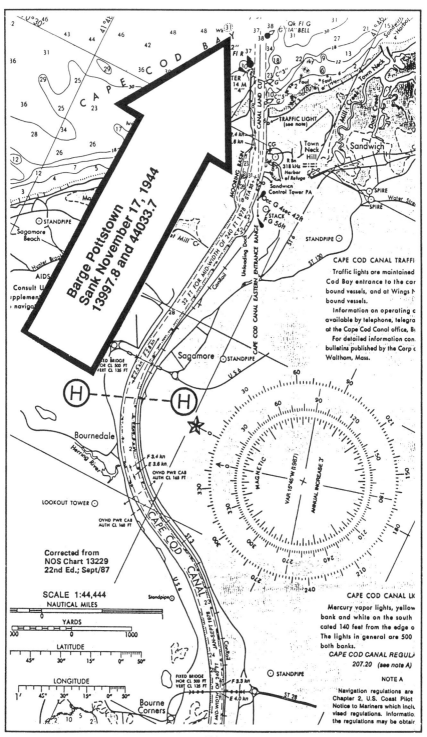

Barge Pottstown
Sank November 17, 1944
13997.8 and 44033.7

CAPE COD BAY

Sandwich

CAPE COD CANAL TRAFFI

Traffic lights are maintained
Cod Bay entrance to the car
bound vessels, and at Wings N
bound vessels.

Information on operating c
available by telephone, telegra
at the Cape Cod Canal office, B
For detailed information con.
bulletins published by the Corp c
Waltham, Mass.

Sagamore

Bournedale

LOOKOUT TOWER

Corrected from
NOS Chart 13229
22nd Ed.; Sept/87

SCALE 1:44,444
NAUTICAL MILES
YARDS
LATITUDE
LONGITUDE

Bourne
Corners

MAGNETIC
VAR 15°45'W (1987)
ANNUAL INCREASE 3'

CAPE COD CANAL LK

Mercury vapor lights, yellow
bank and white on the south
cated 140 feet from the edge o
The lights in general are 500
both banks.

CAPE COD CANAL REGULA
207.20 (see note A)

NOTE A

Navigation regulations are
Chapter 2, U.S. Coast Pilot
Notice to Mariners which inclu
vised regulations. Informatio
the regulations may be obtair

CHAPTER 58

Pottstown

Roughly northeast on a chart showing the Scusset breakwater and the east end of the Cape Cod Canal you'll see a wreck symbol with clearance of 31 feet. There's the final home of the barge Pottstown, sunk November 17, 1944.

The day before the sinking the Red Star Line tug Walthen was coming down the coast with two barges in tow. Rough weather forced her to anchor the Pottstown northeast of the east end while the tug proceeded into the canal with the other one. Both tug and first barge then anchored up at the State Pier until daylight.

During the night the Pottstown developed a leak when her starboard hawse pipe ripped from the hull. Seeing their problem, the crew on the 197 foot barge sent up distress flares to get help from the Coast Guard.

When the captain of the Walthen heard the Pottstown was in trouble he immediately headed his tug back out into Cape Cod Bay. While the crew was in the process of readying a towing hawser, the heavy line slipped over the stern, wrapping in the prop, rendering the tug powerless. Now there were two vessels in distress.

A Coast Guard vessel got the men off the Pottstown in time but she went to the bottom. They then got a line on the tug but on two occasions the tow line parted. Eventually the tug was pushed up on shore where she was broken up by seas after another Coast Guard contingent got the crew off through the surf. Today the remains of the Walthen are in close to shore a short distance north of the Sandwich Public Beach. The Pottstown, after being dynamited in 1945 as a menace to navigation, remains where she sank at 13997.8 and 44033.7.

Cod can be caught around this wreck which might be a good choice if the tide is running to the west in the canal. Usually that's the time to fish other areas until the flow turns east once more. In May, there may or may not be schools of pollock that used to frequent this general location. Pollock, like other New England fish, are not around in the numbers of the past. Declining fish stocks are but one more reason to look to places like wrecks that will still hold some fish in the times in which we live.

Another species likely to frequent the Pottstown are blackfish. We suspect there's fair to good fishing for tautog going untouched here for the angler who can anchor his boat right on the edge of the wreckage then drop a green crab down to see if a ten pounder is hungry. Heavy tackle will be needed to turn the blacks away from the wreck. If they get just a wee bit of slack line they'll dart back into what is their home to cut your line quicker than you can say !#$%&*!!!!.

The passenger steamer Romance was sunk in a collision outside Boston Harbor on September 10, 1936

CHAPTER 59

Romance

If a fisherman were to look over chart 13267 which covers Massachusetts Bay with a loran overlay he would see many wreck symbols in the course of his investigating. One of these can be found by picking up the 13970 line then following it to a point roughly 2-1/2 miles southeast of East Point. When you encounter a wreck cleared to 54 feet you'll have your finger on top of the Romance, sunk September 10, 1936.

The 245 foot long Romance was a wooden passenger steamer that made regular runs from Boston to Providence. On the foggy evening of the 10th, she was getting ready to enter the Boston Harbor approach at President Roads when she was hit on the port side just aft of amidships by the outgoing steamer New York, a much larger vessel.

The sharp bow of the New York sliced far into the Romance but, luckily, the captain of the New York saw the Romance in time to order his engines reversed. Such a maneuver saved his ship from going any further into the Romance than it did and undoubtedly kept some passengers from being crushed. After the collision the captain of the New York kept his ship running forward so the bow stayed into the side of the Romance.

Passengers from the Romance jumped over the deck onto the New York while others climbed up ladders lowered for that purpose. Still others were taken off in lifeboats. By the time the Romance hit bottom only one of her passengers was lost. Four hours after the collision the New York docked at Boston to find waiting ambulances.

Not too long after her sinking, part of the superstructure of the Romance broke free to eventually wash up on Winthrop Beach. The hull and machinery can be found at 13969.4 and 44290.6.

In the spring we think the Romance will be full of school codfish, possibly small pollock which show up in and around Boston Harbor. Close by the Romance are the wrecks of the City of Salisbury, Arco #8, and the Sweet Sue, all of which are covered in other chapters of this book. If Romance is "taken" by another fisherman or dive boat there are other choices on your day off close by.

The summer of 1989, divers inspected the bow of the City of Salisbury to find it full of small cod, red hake and other fish. That year we had very cold water temperatures so the cod stuck around on the wrecks longer than other seasons. If such conditions repeat themselves, look to places like the Romance for a codfish dinner during the summer. What sunk over 60 years ago on a foggy night in September is now a haven for both fish and the fishermen who seek them.

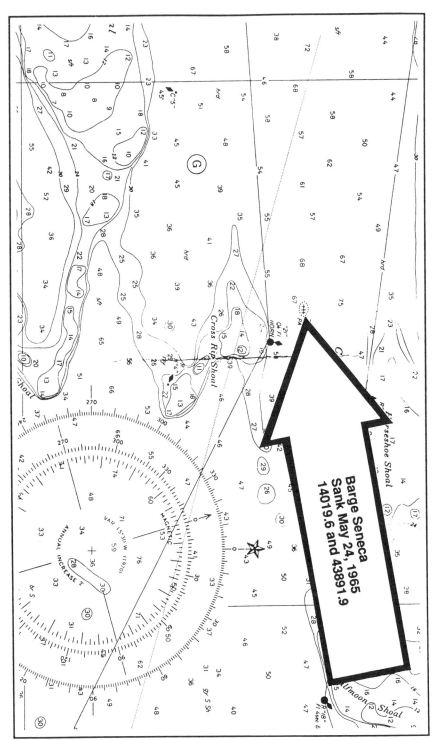

Barge Seneca
Sank May 24, 1965
14019.6 and 43891.9

CHAPTER 60

Seneca

A diver wouldn't give this wreck a second glance for it's just a scow-type barge that sank with a load of stone. But, to a fisherman, the Seneca is now home to some jumbo sea bass, some of them over 5 pounds as witnessed by divers on a trip to 14019.6 and 43891.9 in the summer of 1988.

To several dragger captains this wreck is the Cross Rip stone barge, a location to be avoided for fear of hanging a $5,000 net on something that would not budge. The Seneca came to her role as a hang number on May 24, 1965 as she was being towed with a load of stone for a jetty under construction between Morris and Monomoy Islands. A Notice to Mariners issued the 26th week of that year stated the barge sank 660 yards northwest of Cross Rip Lighted Horn 21 in approximate position of 41-27-05 and 70-17-50. There she sits today, waiting for a hook and line fisherman to come prospecting.

The 126 foot long Seneca is caved in amidships with sand up to her sides in some of those spots. Amidships is also where divers saw the jumbo sea bass eyeing them. Perhaps the sea biscuits were waiting until the divers left before resuming their never-ending search for food. Anglers can take advantage of this need by dropping a diamond jig down dressed with a strip of squid and working it around the edges of the wreck. If sea bass are home they will not let the lure with the nice strip of fresh squid flutter in front of their noses for too long.

A fisherman might also try a hi-lo rig baited with smaller pieces of fresh squid hoping for some scup. The Seneca wreck has them, too. If the spring sea bass run in locations closer to the Cape brings out too much boat traffic for your tastes you could sneak off to the wreck of the Seneca for some elbow room.

Situated where it is in Nantucket Sound, we suspect fluke will be around the wreck also. Try a fluke rig drifted slowly around the bottom on the outskirts of the hull. If you can find some jumbo live killies you have a doormat bait par excellence. If you fancy lures, drop a one to two ounce or heavier bucktail down and work it slowly along the bottom. Your fluke catches will drastically increase if you tip the bucktail with either a strip of squid or a live killie or other baitfish. The bucktail should be just heavy enough to tend bottom. The lightest lure that will stay down during a particular stage of tide is the one that will catch the best.

If you catch a sea robin while fishing, cut the belly strip out of it, then cut the meat into pennant shaped strips. Put one of those on the jig for a tough, long-lasting lure sweetener that will be there after the first fish is in the cooler.

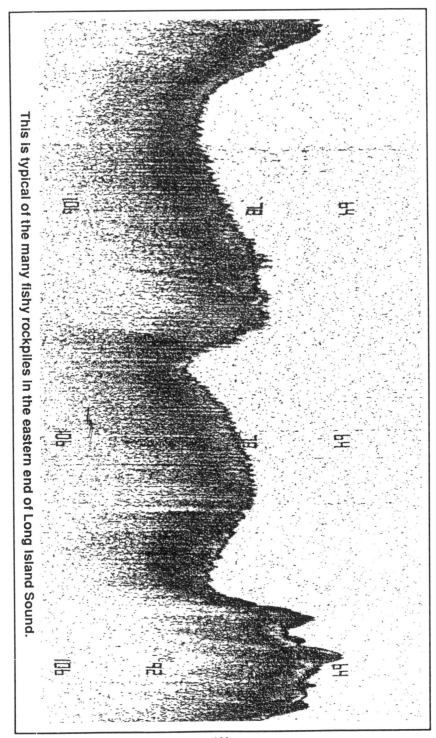

This is typical of the many fishy rockpiles in the eastern end of Long Island Sound.

CHAPTER 61

Sound Numbers, Eastern End

For every one wreck we found in the two years it took to research this book, we probably found four times as many rockpiles or granite "wrecks" as they've been nicknamed by some experienced divers. Here's a rundown of some of the structures we found in our travels on eastern Long Island Sound.

26362.8 and 44002.6
Breakwater Rip. Good location for jigging blues.

26355.1 to 26355.7 and 43991.7 to 43991.8
Outer Southwest Reef area. Rock bottom, good place for scup in summer, tautog in the fall.

26341.8 and 43985.0
East Rip. Bluefishing, both jigging and wire line trolling.

14851.4 and 43985.8
Sharp spike, south of Sand Shoal. Big tide boil overhead. Likely place for blues and some experimentation.

14783.4 and 43973.8
Either deep rockpile or old wreck. Within range of experienced diver to say for sure.

26231.6 and 43981.9
Small rockpile, groundfishing.

26228.2 and 43985.4
Rockpile, scup, tautog, maybe blues.

26226.8 and 43990.3
Rockpile, same as above plus a few large weakfish were caught on these numbers.

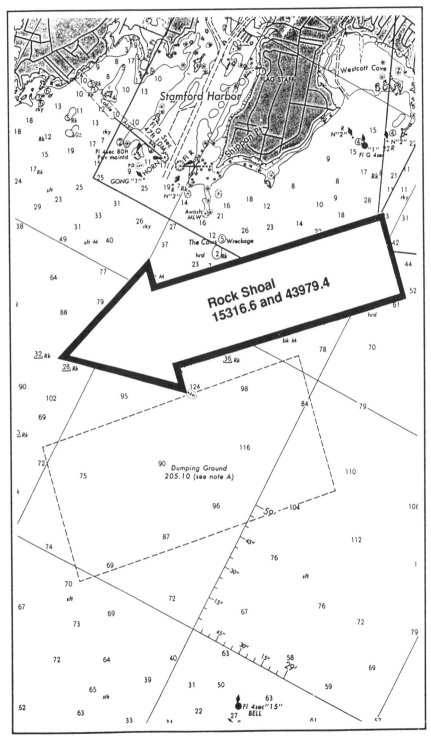

Rock Shoal
15316.6 and 43979.4

CHAPTER 62

Sound Numbers
Western End

During the summer of 1988 the NOAA ship Heck conducted side scan sonar operations in western Long Island Sound. The numbers below are but a part of what the Heck found during those and subsequent trips off the entire Connecticut shoreline. In addition to the work done by the crew of the Heck, a couple of the numbers come to you compliments of divers who wish to remain anonymous.

15186.0 and 43915.6
Smithtown Artificial Reef, groundfish, possible blues.

15316.6 and 43979.4
Rock shoal, blackfishing.

15315.1 and 43978.6
Old schooner wreck close to above, large blackfish.

15315.1 and 43978.9
Inverted wood barge, all of last three structures close together.

15326.5 and 43973.7
Pinnacle Rock, blackfish.

15326.6 and 43973.7
Wood wreck, about 75 feet long, close by Pinnacle Rock, blackfish.

26825.2 and 43993.9
Sailboat wreck on hard bottom, broken up, blackfish.

The remains of the Canadian destroyer St. Francis, formerly the U.S.S. Bancroft, lle off Westport, Ma.

CHAPTER 63

The St. Francis

Similar to the situation with the cruiser U.S.S. Yankee, which lies in nearby Buzzards Bay, very few fishermen are aware that two large warships are on the bottom very close to each other. While this coincidence does not qualify this area as a military graveyard, it does provide a bit of irony. Two vessels which participated in several combat actions in their respective campaigns in the Spanish-American War and World War II came to rest in an area where not a shot was fired in anger.

The Canadian destroyer St. Francis, which is incorrectly referred to as her sister ship the St. Clair in numerous publications, began her life as the U.S.S. Bancroft when she was commissioned in March of 1919. She and her fleet of sister ships were built to combat the German U-boat threat of the first World War but were not completed until after the cease fire was signed.

The Bancroft spent a few years on peacetime duty and was taken out of service in 1922. She was destined for a scrap yard when the Axis launched World War II in 1939 but was sold to the Canadian government to guard convoys. While being towed to a scrap yard after the war she was rammed while operating in dense fog. The old four-stacker sank in about 58 feet of water in one of the most productive bottom fishing areas off Westport, Ma. in mid-July of 1945. She was later cleared as a menace to navigation. Today her scattered and flattened remains can be found at 14307.0 and 43964.6.

Capt. Brad Luther, who has made numerous visits to this popular dive site, reported numerous sightings of tropical and unusual fish such as amberjack, Spanish mackerel, bonito and some large blue sharks as well as the standard bottom fare for this area. On numerous visits to this location over the past two years I have had to pass up fishing as divers had already anchored over the wreckage.

In the spring and fall of the year we have taken some respectable tautog up to 9 pounds, sea bass to 3 pounds along with cunners and loads of pin-size scup. The ship has also produced bluefish between 10 and 12 pounds from August through late October just off the high spot on the bow section which faces north towards Baker's Beach. This past fall we enjoyed some very good fishing when the commercial charter dive boats hadn't claimed the site first.

Along with some very nice summer tautog and sea bass we caught large triggerfish which are battlers to make a tautog fisherman take notice. A lobsterman who has been setting traps along the wreck plates for many years claims he has taken some good catches of scup and sea bass in his traps and reports a fairly regular spring run of mackerel along about mid-May when these fish leave the Newport area and head for the Cape Cod Canal. Although we've never caught one, divers tell us there are some respectable stripers attracted to this wreck by the smorgasbord of feed and cover. If you are able to put a diamond jig past the bluefish you just might interest one of these linesiders.

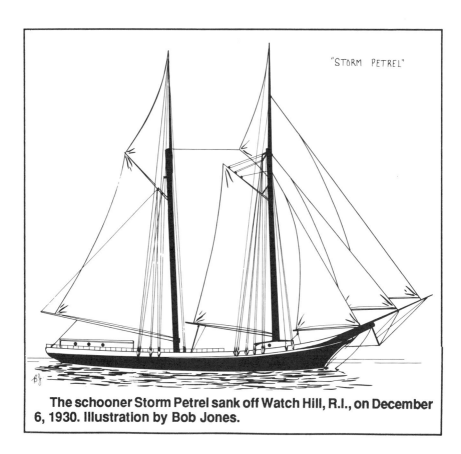

"STORM PETREL"

The schooner Storm Petrel sank off Watch Hill, R.I., on December 6, 1930. Illustration by Bob Jones.

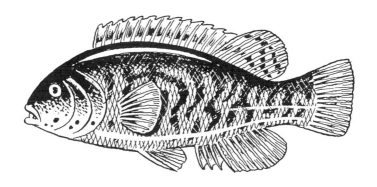

CHAPTER 64

Storm Petrel

Ask a dragger captain from Stonington, Ct. about the better known nearby hangs and he'll likely include the "Negro Schooner" in his choices. Prior to our stumbling onto a newspaper article on the sinking while researching another wreck in the Westerly Public Library, all we could find out was the hang was that of an old schooner that sank near the Watch Hill hooter buoy. All who perished in the sinking were "persons of color".

Over the years draggers pulled up a mast and some old lights when they got too close to the wreck. On at least one occasion a diver had to go down to free a net from the wreckage. The force of time and tide has taken its toll. Today she's a pile of sanded-in debris with only her forward winch giving much of a bottom profile. Her name is the Storm Petrel and she sank while in tow of a Coast Guard vessel on December 6, 1930.

The headline in the Westerly Sun we happened to locate stated that six people lost their lives in a disaster that had its roots two weeks earlier. The Storm Petrel, a ship 100 feet long, left New York bound for Nantucket with a cargo of coal. A day or so later a gale in eastern Long Island Sound tore away her sails. A Coast Guard boat proceeded to tow her to New London but, during the night, the tow line parted. The next day they located the ship aground and once more came to her aid. She eventually made port in New London on November 27, 1930.

While she was in port it became apparent to local shipping interests that the captain had no money and his ship had some liens outstanding. No private towing company would touch the job of taking the leaking vessel to Nantucket, so the Coast Guard, on the evening of December 6, towed the unrepaired Storm Petrel out of the harbor into local legend. Just off the then Watch Hill gas buoy she was, in a short time, severely down by the bow and the next minute gone, taking the captain, his wife, small child and three crew members to their deaths.

Sportfishermen can find the sparse remains of the Negro Schooner at 14643.2 and 43947.3. We'll bet that in time these numbers will be nothing but a pile of sand and a memory to fishing boat captains and readers of this book.

Draggers continue to tow up flounder around the wreck. Codfish will show here in the fall through the spring for the few sportfishing boats on the water after Christmas. Jumbo fluke are also possible targets, especially in September as they make ready to move away from our shores on their annual migration. During the warm months an inquiring angler might locate some deep water tautog seeking relief from higher temperatures on inshore spots.

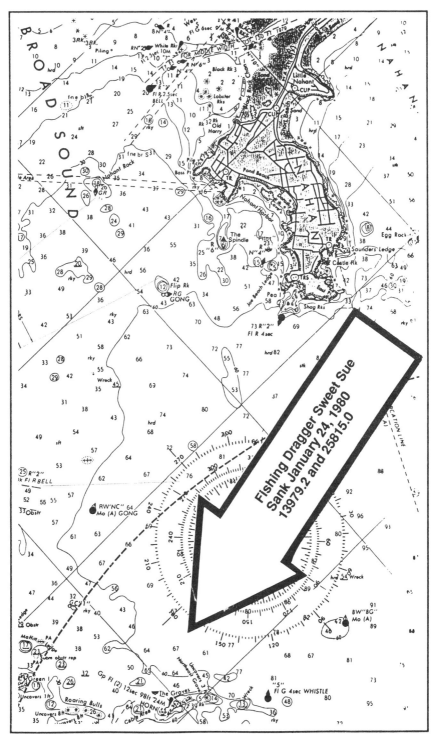

Fishing Dragger Sweet Sue
Sank January 24, 1980
13979.2 and 25815.0

CHAPTER 65

Sweet Sue

If you're one of the many fishermen who fish in and around Boston Harbor, then this wreck is for you. On January 24, 1980 the 47 foot fishing boat Sweet Sue sank in 70 feet of water off Graves Light. Her remains, like the ten thousand ships before her, are now a reef attracting codfish for anglers who drop baited hooks nearby.

The Sweet Sue radioed a request for help to the Coast Guard around midnight on the 23rd. The Coast Guard dispatched a boat from their Woods Hole station but they were unable to locate the stricken dragger at its first reported position to the southeast of Scituate. At first light a helicopter joined the search and they found the Sweet Sue to the north of Scituate. A bum loran was the reason for the foul-up in initial positioning.

After locating her, a cutter took her in tow but she was taking water rapidly through her bow. The copter came over and dropped two pumps to aid the two already in use. From 10 a.m. until 2:25 p.m. the crew fought to hold back the rising waters but it became apparent they would lose their fight. The weather at the time of the foundering was wind gusts to 50 mph and seas from six to eight feet.

The crew were taken off by helicopter then airlifted to Logan Airport in Boston and, from there, to Mass General Hospital for treatment of exposure. Luckily, no one was hurt.

Fishermen running across 13979.2 and 25815.0 can easily see the wreck on their fish finders. School codfish, perhaps in good numbers, hang their hats here until water warms in the summer. If we have a cooler than normal summer you might find small to mid-size cod right through Labor Day. If there are no codfish around we suggest a try for tautog with half of a green crab for bait. Some of the bait shops in the immediate area might not stock green crabs since tautog fishing isn't as widely practiced on the North Shore as it is from Plymouth to the Cape. We suspect, however, there are tautog around that people are not targeting. If anyone does locate some steady tautog fishing on some of the North Shore wrecks, we'd like to hear about your experiences. Just drop us a line care of MT Publications, 2 Denison Avenue, Mystic, CT 06355.

Sherwood Lincoln with a 50 pound cod he jigged up on Tanta's Ledge.

CHAPTER 66

Tanta's Ledge

Roughly 12 miles to the southeast of the Saco River in southern Maine sits not a wreck but an underwater hill that rises from 280 feet to less than 200 feet below the surface of the cold waters of the Gulf of Maine. Here bait fish gather with codfish and other groundfish not far behind. The numbers for some parts of this productive hill are 13360.7 and 25908.4 and 13632.2 and 25911.0. The name of the hill is Tanta's Ledge.

Always worth a stop, particularly during the month of June, this peak is but one of many off the coast of Maine within reach of someone with a small boat. The last time we fished Tanta's we did so on a beautiful Saturday with flat calm seas. Leaving the mouth of the Saco we made the ledge in no time at all in a 20 foot Seacraft center console with 150 hp Yamaha.

We arrived at slack water to find schools of sea herring flipping all over the surface. On our second drift of the day, Sherwood Lincoln landed our third fish; it weighed 50 pounds even. From then until it was time to head for home and the taxidermist we caught 40 more market cod, a great day on the water.

People who wish to follow our steps can do so by launching at the free ramp on the Biddeford side of the Saco River. For directions and overall tips or any tackle you might need we recommend a call to Cal Robinson of Saco Tackle at 207-284-4453. Cal is more than willing to help out-of-staters who come north to sample Maine's codfishing.

We might also mention that the jetties at the mouth of the Saco harbor jumbo stripers. If bass are your game you might throw a couple extra rods in with the cod gear. If the weather is too windy for even the short run offshore you might salvage the day in sheltered waters with linesiders.

All the standard cod jigs will work in Maine. Regular jigging tackle requires 12 ounce jigs on slack water and 14 to 17-1/2 ouncers when the tide is running. People used to fishing for cod off southern New England will find Maine waters a lot deeper closer to shore. You don't have to go far off the coast of Maine to be in 50 fathoms. Speaking of deep water, a friend of ours, Bill Bush from Pine Island, N.Y., makes it a practice to catch cod in super deep water. He uses a standard, heavy action cod rod with 50 pound dacron with jigs from 16 to 26 ounces to fish 400 to 550 feet down, far beyond the limit of most fishermen. He can only do this on days with slow or moderate tides. To date Bill has landed jumbo cusk and steaker cod though not the record he seeks. Bill is convinced a 100 pound codfish awaits his efforts below 60 fathoms. Water of that depth is readily available to the small boat angler not far from Tanta's Ledge.

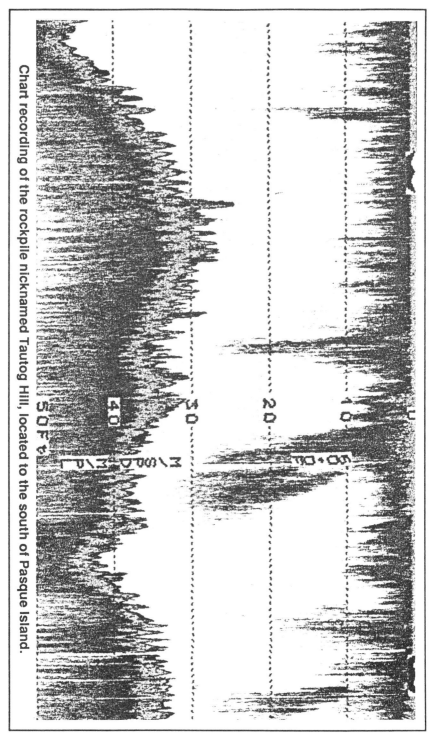

Chart recording of the rockpile nicknamed Tautog Hill, located to the south of Pasque Island.

CHAPTER 67

Tautog Hill

Last summer, on a wreck-hunting expedition which began casually enough with some early morning casting for bass and blues behind the Elizabeth Islands, my guest commented that it was a long time since he had caught a blackfish. Despite my desire to grant his wish, we all knew no self-respecting tautog should be anywhere about as they had all moved into colder and deeper waters. Well, almost all of them. In the fast, cold waters of Vineyard Sound there are a few locations where the chilled water washes the faces of ledges which fall off into deep holes.

Here, along these craggy notches, are concentrations of tautog which have settled in where they have found all the ingredients necessary for their survival. I had taken tog on the backside of the island chain while slow trolling for stripers with a tube and worm rig in mid summer so I knew there were a few around. A third party that day referred to my NOAA chart 13218 and located a steep hill falling off to deeper water very close to the shore on the south side of Pasque Island. It appeared to have all the ingredients necessary for blackfish at 14203.0 and 43930.1.

I made a drift and powered back to set my heavy grapnel ahead of the selected bottom to put us over the notch in the ridge which showed up on the chart paper. After clearing up a few medium scup and some small sea bass, my guest pried a 5 pound blackfish from the face of the hill and the chum pot did the rest. We enjoyed a steady pick of fish ranging from 3 to about 6 pounds until my guest indicated he had enough for his freezer.

Tautog Hill is somewhat of a misnomer. Our initial rip produced a mixed bag of sea bass, scup, and, of course, our fair share of sea robins and choggies. On one trip there in the fall of 1988 I fought a fish for over 5 minutes, all the while entertaining visions of a new state record sea bass, until we saw the white belly and stripes of a 9 or 10 pound linesider that took the sea clam tongue.

I employ a light saltwater bait casting outfit in the 17 to 20 pound range so we carry a large landing net because some fish are too large and feisty to lift with this tackle. This place is quite capable of producing a similar fish of any of the above species.

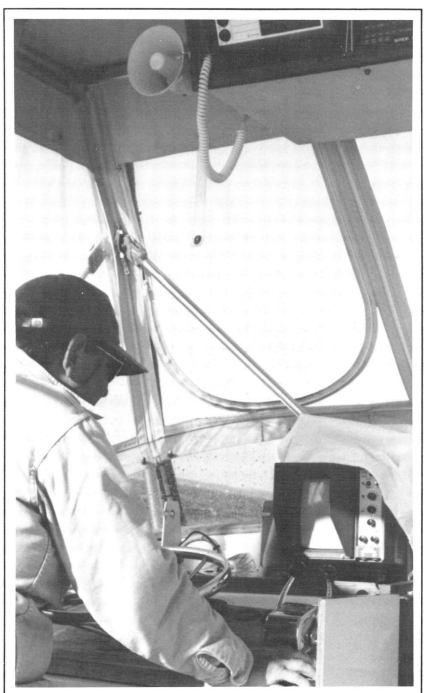

Captain Peter Fisher of the charterboat Fish stares intently at his fish finder while searching for the wreck of the Thames.

CHAPTER 68

Thames

A Notice to Mariners during the 40th week of 1973 stated the 55 foot tug Thames sank in 100 feet of water at position 41-10 and 72-28 in the eastern part of Long Island Sound. That, however, was the only notice of the sinking we could locate. We searched The New York Times, The Westerly Sun and The New London Day but none of those publications had any news whatsoever about the tug.

In 1982 a side scan sonar search by a ship from the National Ocean Service at the above position turned up negative results. However, a target they thought to be the Thames was located at 41-09-19 and 72-25-04. The wreck protruded 9 feet off the bottom in 131 feet of water. In 1983 and 1984 the wreck was cleared to a depth of 73 feet by a wire drag and the depth to bottom was revised to 128 feet down.

Three years after the last wire drag clearance we set out to find the Thames. At first we threw over a marker buoy, then started a systematic grid search. "Fortunately" we did not have enough line on the buoy and it started to wash down with the tide. So, after 15 minutes searching without any results, we went back to retrieve our errant marker. As we steamed up on the jug, there on our color machine appeared our target. Not having enough line on the jug was the best mistake we made all that trip.

You'll locate the wreck of the Thames at 14863.7 and 43955.6. Those bearings came from a Sitex loran on the bridge of Captain Peter Fisher's former 36 foot charterboat Fish. One year later we ran out to the numbers again, but this time used a Raytheon loran on a 20 foot Seacraft owned by Sherwood Lincoln. This time our wreck appeared at 14864.0 and 43955.6, which illustrates the point that even good loran numbers are just an approximation until you pinpoint the wreck with your own machine. Once you have the numbers in your waypoint directory, then you should be able to go right to the tenth and start fishing.

The day our marker jug located the tug for us we saw clouds of bait downtide from the wreck. At the time we didn't take the time to drop a few jigs down to catch some blues but it looked prime for such. Tautog might be around this location and there's the possibility of nice sea bass in the area. Don't forget a drop or two for scup. They might hang around here, too.

This is only a relatively small target so, on a hard tide, it will be tough to stay on. You might mark this as one to hit when the tide eases off or during slack water.

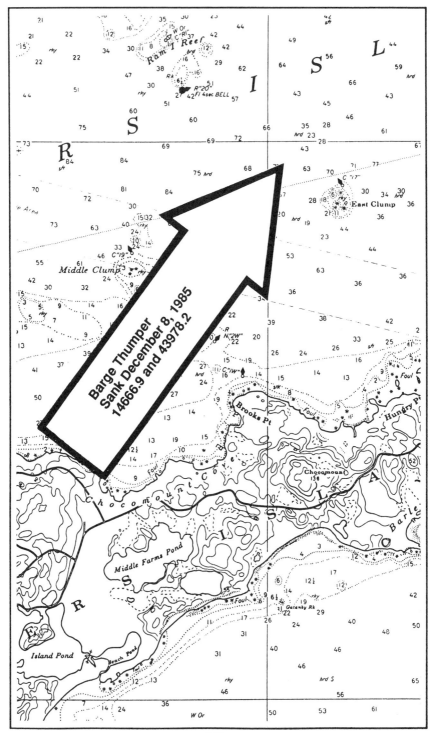

Barge Thumper
Sank December 8, 1985
14666.9 and 43978.2

CHAPTER 69

Thumper

On December 8, 1985 the commercial trawler Neptune was towing the Thumper, a 40 by 20 foot wooden barge with a pile driving crane atop it, from Barrington, R.I. to Westbrook, Ct., on Long Island Sound. They'd left Barrington the day before to spend the night in Point Judith, leaving there about 5:30 on the morning of the eighth. They expected to reach Westbrook late that afternoon.

As the trawler and barge got in Fisher's Island Sound, between East Clump and Ram Island, the barge suddenly started taking on water through a starboard baffle. Once that happened, it tilted to one side, then sank. It took all of three minutes from the time the two crew members noticed something was wrong until the barge sank out from under them.

When the barge went down, the crew on the trawler let go the tow line so their vessel wouldn't be pulled under, then came about to pick up the two bargemen in the water without survival suits. The water temperature at the time was in the high 40s. After being pulled aboard the Neptune, the two men were transferred to a 41 foot Coast Guard boat that rushed them to waiting ambulances at a nearby marina for transfer to a hospital in New London, Ct. Though one man spent the night in intensive care, both survived their ordeal.

Today the barge and the debris that fell off it can be located in the area of 14666.9 and 43978.2 to 14667.0 and 43977.7. To find the crane, scout the bottom a short jog to the west of these bearings.

Scup set up housekeeping around the Thumper in 80 feet of water. Some flats can be caught around the edges of the debris while tautog can be anywhere they feel safe. If you fish the Thumper late in the fall, say around mid to late November, you might catch a tautog over 10 pounds. If it's too windy to go outside of Fisher's Island, you have wrecks like this and the Marise or the Blackfish Schooner to salvage one more day before the boat goes away for the season. If we have a better fluke season than 1989, check the area around the Thumper for doormats.

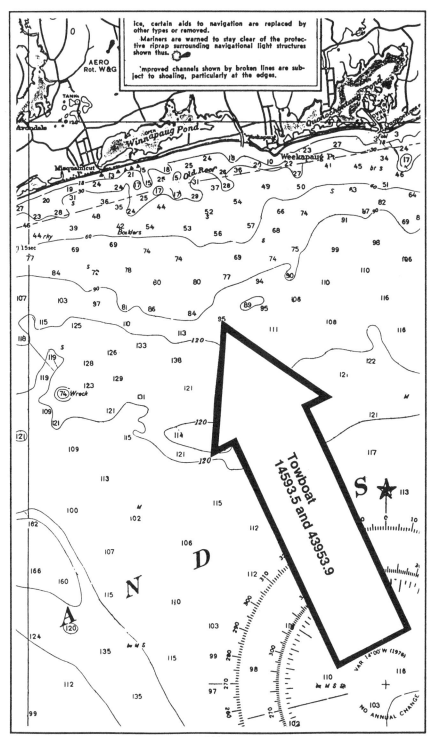

CHAPTER 70

The Towboat

Not far off the shores of Misquamicut, R.I., sits an unknown. We know what type of ship it was, where it's located, but not the name nor history. At 14593.5 and 43953.9 fishermen can locate a wreck identified by divers as a tug and nicknamed the towboat by local dragger captains.

When we first started researching this wreck we were told this was the tug Hercules, sunk in December, 1907, but a check of local newspaper archives showed that vessel ran up on the beach after striking a submerged object. A very experienced local diver, after we informed him of our findings, said there's a shallow wreck in close to shore where the Hercules went ashore. Our old diver friend thinks that's the Hercules.

Other sources said the tug was called Stormy Weather which sent us back to the newspaper files. There we found two boats called Stormy Weather. The first ran aground on the south shore of Rhode Island on January 18, 1950. She was a fishing boat, not a tug. In the end she was burned where she lay. The second Stormy Weather was another fishing boat, sunk on April 4, 1974, approximately five miles from Montauk Point. It would seem neither of those fit the bill.

Noted marine historian Jim Jenney, formerly from Saunderstown, R.I., guessed this might be the lost tug William Maloney. In November, 1924, the Maloney set out from Brooklyn, N.Y., bound for Newport, R.I. Somewhere along the way she sank and, according to Jim, the crew disappeared. The vessel's sinking was followed by a tricky "insurance thing" that didn't sit quite right.

To Jim's research on the Maloney we can add that the previous year the tug sat at a Coast Guard yard reserved for "blacks," the nickname given to vessels caught smuggling liquor into the country during Prohibition. We couldn't locate further references to the Maloney after 1923 but it doesn't take much to wonder if the tug was again up to her old ways when she disappeared. Time and more research will tell.

Our unknown tug sits in 95 feet of water and comes up 8 feet off the bottom. Blackfish come around in the spring through the fall as do scup in the summer. Fluke no doubt move through from time to time, stopping off where there's a meal to be had. Codfish, too, would like this wreck if they migrate in good numbers up into Block Island Sound as they used to in years past. If there's bait, the blues will investigate the towboat as they move through on their way south in the fall. When you drop a lure or bait down on a wreck you just never know what awaits.

The freighter Trojan was sunk off Martha's Vineyard on January 20, 1906. Photo courtesy of the Peabody Museum of Salem, Ma.

CHAPTER 71

Trojan

The term graveyard, when applied to the area between Cuttyhunk and Gay Head, has been well deserved. When you combine the hazardous approaches of Devil's Bridge on the south and Sow and Pigs on the north, you are talking about some formidable rockpiles. When the diverging water temperatures merge with their rotary currents, you have a combination that produces what local mariners refer to as black fog. Those thick, impenetrable walls of heavy moisture have contributed to putting many a good ship on the bottom.

The steel cargo steamer Trojan was barely making headway in dense fog at 11:00 a.m. on January 20, 1906 when she was rammed amidships on her port side by the passenger steamer Nacoochee enroute from Savannah, Ga. to Boston. The Trojan was a 260 foot steel hull with a 38.4 foot beam and draft of 23.5 feet. She was carrying a valuable cargo of general freight which she took to the bottom with her. The collision was so violent and without warning there was no chance to put the boats over. The men immediately headed for the rigging as the ship began to sink due to the huge gash which let sea water flood her bilges and snuff out her boilers in less than 30 seconds. That the Nacoochee's captain and crew pulled off a rescue of the Trojan's entire crew of 27 men without a loss or serious injury was considered just short of miraculous, given the black fog and winter conditions.

Due to the depth of the water there was never any attempt to salvage the steamer, but divers took off tons of bronze ingots and other valuable souvenirs in the early 1970's. The remains of the ship lie in 110 feet of water at 14291.4 and 43921.4 on fairly level mud bottom and present a very good profile on the chart recorder.

The hull is open in several locations providing excellent cover for bait fish and marine growth while her proximity to Sow and Pigs and Gay Head reefs makes her attractive to species such as striped bass, which divers report seeing in fair numbers amid her ruins along with tautog, scup and codfish in spring and fall. Bluefish take over from mid-July through late October. Fish up to 14 pounds were taken by a passenger on my boat but it's quite possible to get your lure or bait through them and down to the bottom feeders.

A trip here in August of 1989, using both sea clams and two-hook bottom fish rigs as well as diamond jigs of assorted weights spiced with squid and fish attractant, produced tautog, scup, sea bass, dogfish and a striped bass of 12 pounds which caused a bit of excitement because we believed we were fighting a potential world record sea bass.

The wreck is foul, so you'll lose a lot of rigs. A diver who frequents this location searching for bronze ingots and assorted bottles from her cargo, which included barrels of soda and whiskey, crates of bottles, bags of wool and assorted rope, glassware and miscellaneous freight, reported several large pieces of nylon dragger net and pieces of gill net which capture lures and rigs. The potential for excellent catches, though, outweighs the loss of a few pieces of gear.

Lola Soares with a jumbo sea bass caught off the wreck of the Uncle John. This was the largest sea bass entered in the Massachusetts Saltwater Fishing Derby in 1988.

CHAPTER 72

Uncle John

At the outermost entrance of this historic fishing port, approximately one mile northwest of the #1 fairway buoy, are the remains of an old Navy patrol boat converted to the hard life of a dragger. The Uncle John was on her way home, making her way through the west end of the Cape Cod Canal at the height of a howling storm late in the day of November 13, 1947.

Six foot seas and winds up to 80 miles per hour were reported as the storm wracked the coastline leaving destruction in its path. The 110 foot wooden vessel labored into Buzzards Bay around noon, by nightfall she was on the bottom. The crew reported that she sank so fast they only had time to jump over the side with the clothes on their backs. The fishing vessel California heard their mayday and came to the stricken ship's rescue. The crew agreed that if it were not for their rescuer they would never have survived this winter hurricane in the 30 foot seine boat in which they took refuge.

Since that first time when her distinct profile was etched across the paper of our chart recorder, she has provided us with some memorable and rewarding trips. Our initial trip indicated this was a preferred location for one of my favorite bottom feeding species, the black sea bass, as well as a hangout for large bluefish that feed on the bait fish attracted to her structure. The wreck lies at 14200.0 and 43970.1. adjacent to some large rocks which are occasionally mistaken for her remains.

After taking a number of medium sea bass and mostly undersized scup that first evening, we returned the following day and my wife boated sea bass of 4 pound, 8 ounces and 5 pounds, 2 ounces that were certified on a New Bedford fish house's scales. Using sea clams and sea bass rigs on subsequent trips we had doubles of scup and sea bass, tautog and several halves of the aforementioned when bluefish were in residence. The wreck produces some tautog but not in numbers perhaps due to the fact that there are a number of very productive blackfish ledges nearby.

This wreck is not a location you'll want to fish in fog or limited visibility as the New Bedford fishing fleet constantly steams in and out of this busy port very close to the wreck site. I would also caution anyone against double-anchoring or locking into the side of the wreck via grapnel due to the steep boat wakes encountered.

Last season, in July, sea bass fishing was sporadic at best until a few good-sized humpbacks moved into the area. When sloppy conditions offshore forced us to try her again in late summer we enjoyed a good bite which produced the big fish for my wife. That fish proved to be the Bay State Governor's Cup winner for all divisions for 1988 and earned her a silver bowl. You won't find many fish this size on the Uncle John but it's a great alternate location when weather keeps you close to shore.

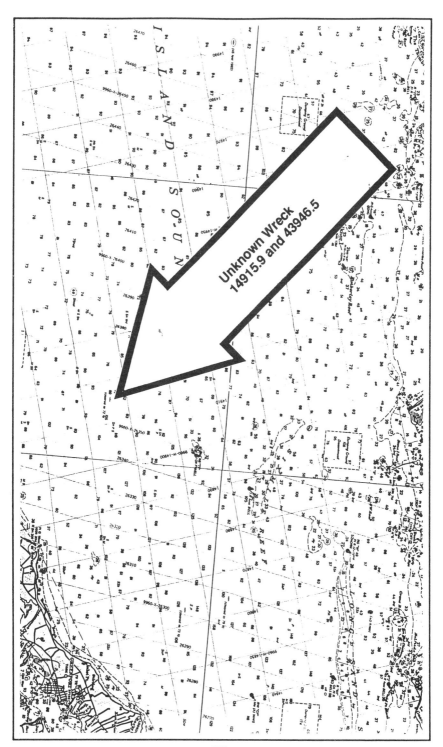

Unknown Wreck
14915.9 and 43946.5

CHAPTER 73

Unknown

There's not too much we can say about this one except that it's an unknown wreck located in the eastern part of Long Island Sound. The wreck list from the National Ocean Service had it listed off Duck Pond Point at position 41-06-45 and 72-32-10.

At one point in this wreck's past she was cleared to a depth of 72 feet for any deep draft ships that might run over her. At this point that's all we know about her, except the date we located it. On October 29, 1987, we found our target for that day at 14915.9 and 43946.5.

From the looks of this wreck on a color fish finder we'd guess it to be one more barge that never made port. We said barge because it looks kind of "boxy," an elongated U-shape resting on a flat bottom in about 90 feet of green Long Island Sound water. The identity of this wreck waits for a diver inquisitive enough to spend his day off poking for clues.

Tautog will be around this one from time to time as well as scup. Don't overlook the possibility of some big sea bass taking a squid strip or other bait meant for porgies. Though caught by accident most of the time, sea bass are around in catchable numbers. Among the prime spots for sea bass, be it inshore or outside in the ocean, are shipwrecks. During the summer and early fall, though, we suspect few people take aim specifically at the sea biscuits, despite the fact they are good eating and grow to six-plus pounds. Like shipwreck fishing, sea bass fishing in the Sound is another overlooked aspect of the world's best sport.

The Vineyard Lightship was sunk in a hurricane on September 14, 1944. Photo courtesy of the National Archives.

CHAPTER 74

Vineyard Lightship

On September 14, 1944 a terrible hurricane swept over the New England coast. During the height of the storm, residents of Westport, Ma. saw bright lights illuminating the inky sky. At first no one could explain the strange lights but afterwards it became clear those were distress signals from the men aboard the Vineyard Sound Lightship anchored to the west of Cuttyhunk Island; those lights were the last messages from doomed seamen.

Because of wartime security all the Coast Guard said five days after the incident was that the 112 foot, iron ship was off station. We might assume the authorities weren't sure at first if the ship was the victim of nature or a torpedo from a prowling U-boat. Eleven days after the sinking, Navy divers located the wreck but it wasn't until September of 1963 when private individuals did so. Captain Brad Luther of the Fairhaven Divers' Club, with help from Professor Edgarton from the Massachusetts Institute of Technology, using an early version of the side scan sonar, located the ship in 65 feet of water three miles west of Cuttyhunk.

Subsequent dives by Captain Luther and others determined that the five ton storm anchor hadn't been lowered as was the procedure during severe weather. Instead, it was surmised, the anchor broke free of her lashings to beat against the bow plates until they gave way and took on water. Today the remains of the lightship can be found at 14289.6 and 43931.3.

Divers told us they've seen enormous tautog on this wreck during July. Rod and reel fishermen have caught them -- to date -- to 9 pounds but larger fish can be expected as more people fish this shipwreck. Hook and line anglers can also catch bluefish of various sizes; scup in summer, some sea bass, fluke around the edges of the hull, possibly some small cod during the winter months and stripers from time to time.

The blues will hit diamond jigs if they're feeding in midwater or chunks of fresh pogy fished on the bottom if that's where their food is that particular day. Divers also told us they've seen large stripers around the deteriorated hull so fresh chunk bait may provide more than just bluefish. Most of the local dragger captains have numbers on this hang so the fluke will have a sanctuary of sorts. Cunners abound at times on the lightship which means a squid strip meant for fluke will have to get by the "perch" before a doormat can nail it.

If the codfish stocks improve to the point where anglers in southern New England can once again catch cod in good numbers close to shore, the lightship wreck will increase in value. As it is situated now, it's a perfect stopover for whatever fish move in and out of Buzzards Bay as well as the fisherman or woman coming in a small boat from a variety of marinas or launch ramps from Sakonnet, R.I. to New Bedford, Ma.

The wreck of the U.S.S. Yankee lies off Round Hill near South Dartmouth, Ma. Photo courtesy of the Naval Historical Center.

CHAPTER 75

Yankee

How many fishermen know that less than five miles away from the busy Massachusetts port of New Bedford and the small boat launching ramp at South Dartmouth lies the wreck of the 391 foot Navy auxiliary cruiser, the U.S.S. Yankee? Today the Yankee wreck is roughly a 400 x 100 foot reef in 45 feet of water, home to game and groundfish.

The Yankee started life as a luxury liner but, in 1898, was purchased by the U.S. Government for duty as a patrol and troop ship during the Spanish-American War. After the war she served in various capacities. On September 23, 1908 she was serving as a training ship off the coast of Massachusetts when she ran aground on Spindle Rock, a part of Hen and Chickens Reef not far from the town of Westport. A private salvager succeeded in floating the ship, then got her almost to New Bedford but the stress on her hull from the towing caused her to sink once again, this time east of Great Ledge just off Round Hill in South Dartmouth.

In time most of the ship's superstructure was removed, then she was dynamited to keep her from becoming a threat to other vessels in this busy approach to New Bedford, home to a large fishing fleet.

Most of the wreck is flattened and scattered, though portions of the bow and stern rise eight feet off the bottom. Divers found a dragger's net hung on one side of the wreckage. That's interesting since there hasn't been any dragging allowed in this region for years. The correct numbers for the Yankee are 14205.6 and 43975.9. She holds scup, sea bass, tautog, choggies, some school bass and bluefish.

The blues can be caught by trolling, sometimes with as little as 75 feet of wire line. You could use any of the standard bluefish trolling lures such as an umbrella rig or a bunker spoon. At times you'll mark the blues atop the wreck in midwater while on other trips you'll find them down near the bottom. At still other times there are no bluefish at all.

Some days a school bass might take a half of a green crab fished for tautog. On other tides, sea bass will dart out from the wreckage to nail a piece of bait just like the ambush of a bluefish. If you're lucky enough to get away from the hordes of choggies that live around the Yankee you could do very well with sea bass from small specimens to jumbos. Eager fishermen bait up with pieces of fresh squid here rather than sea clams since squid will stay on the hook longer after the choggies start pecking away at your bait. Some days the activity of the choggies around your bait draws the attention of larger sea bass which swim in to grab the offering away from the pesky bait stealers.

About the Author

Tim Coleman has fished from different beaches, rockpiles, private and partyboats since he was six. He's made a lot of life's decisions based on the need to be near the water. His interest in angling was interrupted for service in Vietnam and, afterwards, a B.A. degree in journalism from the University of Rhode Island.

The love of fishing led him to his present job as managing editor of *The New England Fisherman*. Besides his work for *The Fisherman*, he's also a free-lance writer and accomplished photographer. His credits include *Outdoor Life, The Long Island Fisherman, Salt Water Fisherman, The New Jersey Fisherman, Garcia Fishing Annual, Pennsylvania Angler, Mercury Marine's Outdoors* and *Florida Fishing News*.

About the Author

Charley Soares is an avid fisherman, hunter and naturalist who has lived all of his life along the coast, fishing from the Gulf of Maine to Florida. Over the past 25 years he has shared his experiences and information through the pages of local, regional and national publications. He has been on *The Fisherman* staff since 1975 and writes the Boating Angler column for the Fisherman Group. He is Salt Water Editor of *New England Out of Doors* and his credits include *The National Fisherman, Small Boat Journal, Salt Water Sportsman* and *Offshore*. He is a Massachusetts Marine Fisheries Commissioner, currently working under a grant from the Massachusetts Arts Lottery Council on a maritime history project.

Acknowledgements

Mark Friese and Meg Moore, National Ocean Service
Captain Brad Luther
The New York Times
"The Source"
Connecticut College Microfilm Library
The Westerly Sun
Stanley Kalbus, Naval Historical Center
National Archives
The Boston Globe
The Peabody Museum
Captain Joe Rendeiro
Mystic Seaport Museum
The Boston Herald
Anonymous Divers and Fishermen
Captain Arthur Medeiros
The Quincy Patriot Ledger
Quincy Public Library
Professor Henry Keatts
Mr. Arnold Carr
The New London Day
Mr. Pete Koutrakis
The Mariners Museum
The Steamship Historical Society
Mr. Bob Jones, Eagle's Nest Studio
Captain Frank Blount
Master Diver Bill Campbell
Mr. John Raguso

Special thanks goes to
Elizabeth Coleman
Research Director

Acknowledgements

The Westerly Public Library
The Plymouth Public Library
Captain Roger Jarvis
Captain Joseph Avilla
Mrs. Gladys Mack, Bayville Historical Society
Officer Richard Taracka
Mr. Lada Simek
Mr. Ron Brissette
The Boston Public Library
Mr. William Quinn, Author
Captain Peter Fisher
Mr. Cal Robinson
Mr. Bill Bush
Mr. Stan Schwartz
Mr. Sherwood Lincoln
Captain Dennis Sabo
Captain Ron Ward
Mr. Luciano Bellastrini
Mr. Steven Lang, Tugboat Research
Steve Cryan Studio
Mr. Craig Lorenzo
Mr. Charley Wolf
Mr. Paul Morris
Dr. Frank Bush
Mr. Frank DeLeo
The Noank Historical Society
The Army Corps of Engineers
Mr. Jim Jenney, Marine Historian
Captain Fred Gallagher
Mrs. Gloria Najim
Unsinkable Mary Motherway